For the Smith and Watson families, whose endu
the creation of these kinds of t

An infographic history of Germany, 1918-45

Conal Smith
&
Elliott L. Watson

Published by New Spur Publishing

First published 2020

For permission requests, please contact us at www.versushistory.com, elliottlwatson74@gmail.com, and prohistoricman@gmail.com.

Websites
www.versushistory.com
www.thecourseworkclub.com

Twitter:
@VersusHistory
@thelibrarian6
@prohistoricman

Instagram:
versushistory

Foreword by Kate Jones

For Germany, the 20th century was certainly turbulent to say the least. The period 1918-45 continues to attract attention, interest and intrigue from students, teachers, historians and the general public alike. People are simply fascinated with the dramatic rise and fall of the Nazi regime. The origins, growth and advancement of the Third Reich is, however, complex. There was a fabric of events, happening both inside and outside Germany, woven together to pave the way for Hitler to gain control as Der Führer. Once in control, Hitler and his National Socialists transformed most aspects of life in Germany. Despite the complexities of this period, *an infographic history of Germany 1918-45* does exactly what the authors intend as it provides a simple solution for the reader to gain insight, understanding and wisdom. The simple solution to fully grasping the key events, turning points and vocabulary of the period is achieved with ease and sophistication on every page.

There are an extraordinary number of books available that detail Germany from 1918-45, many of which are referred to and recommended throughout *an infographic history of Germany 1918-45*, but Smith and Watson have achieved something unique and remarkable. The infographics created in this book are of such a high quality – both in content and design. They are clear, concise, chronological and colourful! It is evident that each infographic has been carefully considered, taking the complex and making it simple to comprehend, which isn't always easy with this topic. Each infographic contains essential information, covering a wide range of events focusing on dates, bite-size summaries, useful visuals and some truly shocking statistics! The research from cognitive science informs us that when information is combined through visual images and texts, often referred to as dual coding, it can help us to encode, understand and remember that information with greater ease. The infographics will serve as a great revision resource to students studying Germany whether that be at Key Stage Three, GCSE, A Level/IB or even Further Education. As a teacher and Head of History I have already envisioned how the infographics can be used to support my teaching practice and I have planned to download the quality infographics to create a visually impressive and historically rich classroom display. Readers of this book outside of education will also no doubt greatly appreciate the layout, design and historical content of every single infographic.

The infographics are further complemented by the accompanying text which provide another layer of depth, detail and discussion for the reader. There is a great narrative of events running through the book but it also goes beyond a merely descriptive account. Students often make the mistake of assuming that the study of History relies primarily on the of recalling dates. Whilst chronology is an important aspect, a skill that can be difficult to grasp is an awareness of significance. Each infographic is accompanied by a superb summary of significance which supports the reader in their comprehension of the impact of every decision, event and outcome.

In addition to the contextual overview is the inclusion of historiography, so often neglected or absent in many texts. There are quotes offering insights and descriptions from leading historians in this field such as Ian Kershaw and Richard J Evans, in addition to many other academics. As someone interested in this period, both professionally and personally, I am now inspired to carry out further exploration and can do so based on the substantial recommended reading, watching and listening provided in each section. I will be ordering many of the texts included in this book for the school and department library. I will also refer back to this book to guide and encourage my students to read more widely based on the trustworthy suggestions by the accomplished and knowledgeable authors.

This truly is a book that keeps on giving; I was surprised and delighted to find an all-encompassing glossary of key terms provided too! This book is drenched in sophisticated vocabulary, take for example 'gleichschlatung' or 'Großdeutschland', and there are many terms used throughout the book that are specific to this period. The reader may or may not be familiar with this terminology but they will certainly gain a confident awareness after reading this book. This is a book I, and I am sure many readers, will return to again and again. *an infographic history of Germany 1918-45* by Smith and Watson truly is an immersive, fascinating and visually stunning read.

Kate Jones.

Pages of history:

Writing history

History is not neat. Human activity is messy; the recording of it is almost as messy. History is a woven web of infinite strands that requires the greatest of efforts not only to identify those strands but also to trace them in a manner that sensibly, honestly and truthfully shows their connections. Many students of History do not ever come close to fathoming their way through this web of human interaction; very few can say they have successfully identified the individual filaments; even fewer can claim to have understood the entire fabric. How then can we students make sense of something so seemingly inscrutable? Perhaps a complex problem requires a simple solution.

When schools and universities teach the subject of History, they tend to do so by delineation: they find ways to classify and categorise; dividing and subdividing information into consumable, understandable, 'chunks'. The learner is then more readily able to understand the history being taught. Issues of cause, consequence, and significance are often explored through such delineations precisely because they are *easier* to deliver and assimilate. It is through these selected delineations – of which there are many (time period, theme, rise/fall and so on) – that the interminably complex weave of the infinite number of contributing factors affecting how History is perceived and recorded, can be understood. Since History cannot always be measured in the same way the Natural Sciences are able to measure the physical world, perhaps the way forward is to, *at first*, simplify. Once simplified and understood, students of History can then take their understanding of a topic and build upon it – the way an intricately-designed house might be constructed upon the most rudimentary of foundations. Our book was written to accomplish this very end.

Every other page of *an infographic history of Germany 1918-45* contains a freely downloadable high-quality infographic that distils some of the details of key issues within the history of this period. Each infographic is accompanied on the opposite page by an overview of the issue being dealt with, a sophisticated (but brief) explanation as to its significance, an example of historiography which has been selected for its thought-provoking and enlightening nature, as well as some suggestions for further exploration of the topic.

The infographic opposite (which can be downloaded using the QR Code on this page) is an example of how a significant stretch of complex history can be 'delineated' via theme and time-period. We try our best to do something similar for each area of German history covered in this book.

We hope it helps in some way.

A big thank you to Kate Jones for writing the foreword to this book and for being a constant source of support.

Conal & Elliott

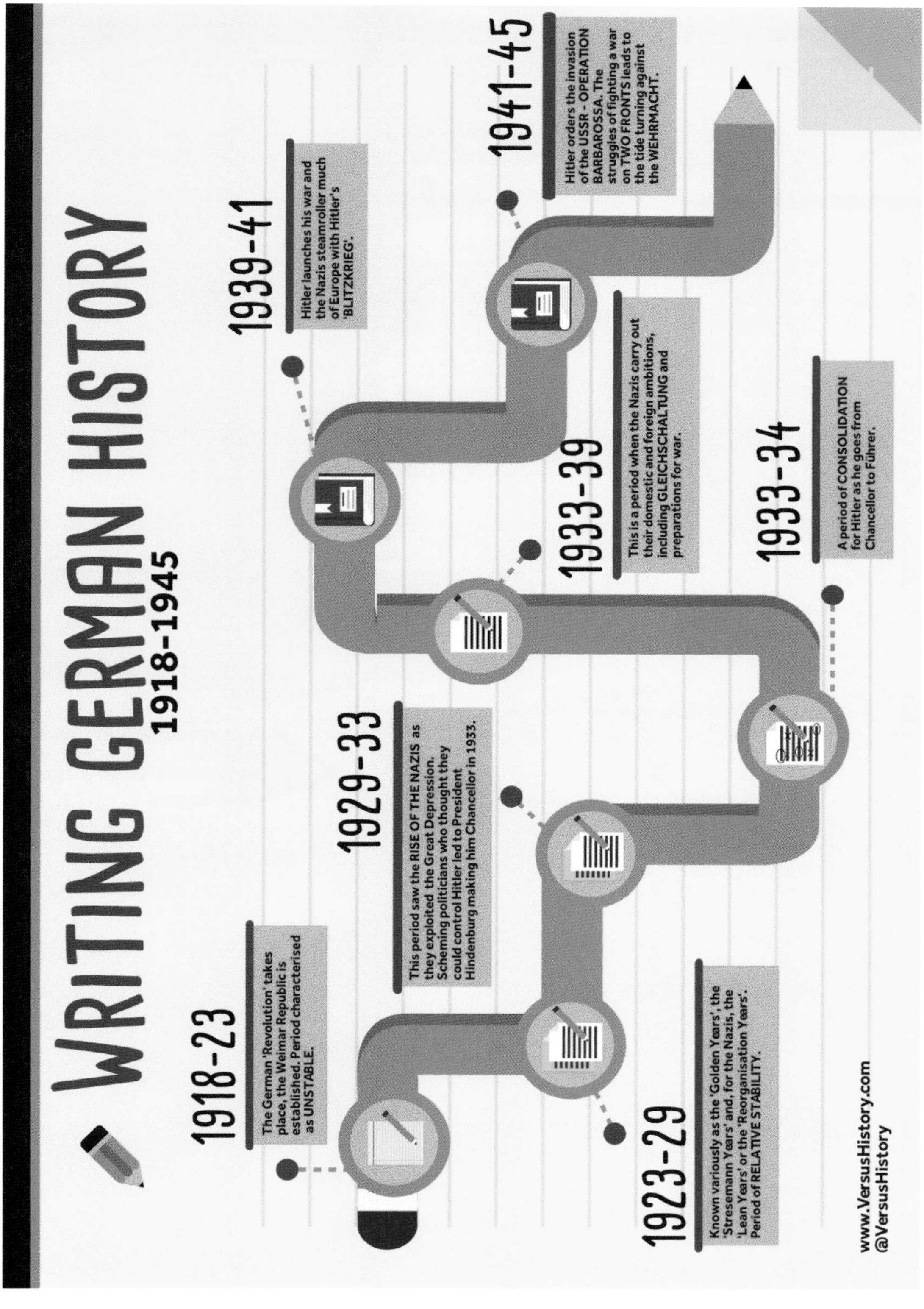
WRITING GERMAN HISTORY
1918-1945
1918-23
The German 'Revolution' takes place, the Weimar Republic is established. Period characterised as UNSTABLE.
1923-29
Known variously as the 'Golden Years', the 'Stresemann Years' and, for the Nazis, the 'Lean Years' or the 'Reorganisation Years'. Period of RELATIVE STABILITY.
1929-33
This period saw the RISE OF THE NAZIS as they exploited the Great Depression. Scheming politicians who thought they could control Hitler led to President Hindenburg making him Chancellor in 1933.
1933-34
A period of CONSOLIDATION for Hitler as he goes from Chancellor to Führer.
1933-39
This is a period when the Nazis carry out their domestic and foreign ambitions, including GLEICHSCHALTUNG and preparations for war.
1939-41
Hitler launches his war and the Nazis steamroller much of Europe with Hitler's 'BLITZKRIEG'.
1941-45
Hitler orders the invasion of the USSR - OPERATION BARBAROSSA. The struggles of fighting a war on TWO FRONTS leads to the tide turning against the WEHRMACHT.
www.VersusHistory.com
@VersusHistory

1918-23
Weimar instability

A number of problems

Overview

The Great War of 1914-1918 was the most destructive war the world had ever seen, involving and influencing a greater number of people and their countries than any in history. Despite Germany being one of the original belligerents in the conflict, the stalemate of trench warfare swiftly brought any notion that this German campaign would be resolved by Christmas and in Germany's favour, to a screeching halt. In fact, the combined might (both military and economic) of the Allies – Britain and her Empire, France, Russia, the United States, and Italy – ultimately brought the Imperial German Army to its knees. More than this, wartime demands that were forced upon the civilians of Germany – from famine to poverty – meant that, long before the war was brought to an end, the Kaiserreich was crumbling.

Significance

Both the short and long-term consequences of the war were formative for Germany and her people. In almost every respect – politically, economically, socially, militarily, geographically, as well as existentially – World War One reshaped what Germany would look like after it was over. From the abdication of the Kaiser, the installation of an unfamiliar democratic model, to the universally despised Treaty of Versailles, the rise of extremist political entities, and a renaissance in German culture and art, nothing in Germany would ever be the same. The impact of World War One also helped sow the seeds of a second, even more devastating, conflict: World War Two.

Historiography

"The Allied blockade policy against Germany…increased population loss and spread death and disease, as famine encroached upon the civilian populations of Central Europe. Its prolongation by the Allies after the cease-fire was intended as a strategy to prevent the resurgence of German military power…"

N.P. Howard

The Social and Political Consequences of the Allied Food Blockade of Germany 1918-19

Where to find out more

Weimar Germany: Promise and Tragedy
Eric D. Weitz

World War One: A Short History
Norman Stone

IMPACT OF WW1 ON GERMANY:
FACTS
@VersusHistory
VersusHistory.com
750,000
CIVILIAN DEATHS
British naval blockade caused starvation among civilian population
2 MILLION SOLDIERS DEAD
4 MILLION SOLDIERS WOUNDED
Gov't debt trebled to:
150
billion marks
1,700
Berliners die of influenza on one day in September 1918
400,000
Berliners go on strike, January 1918
c'40,000
Sailors, soldiers and workers mutiny in Kiel, calling for '"peace and bread"
On the 9th November 1918, it was announced that the Kaiser had abdicated. The next day he boarded a train to the Netherlands, never to return. Was this a 'revolution'?

A killing joke

Overview

When Germany signed the Armistice in the early hours of November 11th, 1918, it set the country on a course towards a reckoning. That reckoning would come the following year on 28th June, with the signing of the Treaty of Versailles. The treaty was shaped primarily by the 'Big Three': Georges Clemenceau of France, David Lloyd George of Britain, and Woodrow Wilson of the United States. Each of these men had vastly different visions of what the post-war world should look like, with Wilson championing *collective security* and *national self-determination*, whereas Clemenceau looked to a punitive outcome and the creation of a European continent absent of any significant German power. The completed treaty was forced upon the new German government, who had no other option but to sign it.

Significance

The terms of the treaty were so damaging to Germany and her people that their impact would be felt for decades. More than this, the Versailles settlement, described by eminent contemporary British economist, John Maynard Keynes, as containing *"...in it much that is unjust and much more that is inexpedient... The new states we are setting up cannot survive in such surroundings"*, would help cause traumas across Europe, that would echo throughout the Twentieth Century. Some historians see the treaty as being the single-most significant contributing factor to the rise of German extremism and a second world war; others, however, see it merely as a context within which individuals played the larger roles.

Historiography

"The public adulation the President (Woodrow Wilson) experienced in Paris... reaffirmed his conviction that he alone carried the hopes of the world's masses for a peaceful and progressive world order. The vision was glorious; the realities, less so".

Norman A. Graebner & Edward M. Bennett
The Versailles Treaty and its Legacy: The Failure of the Wilsonian Vision

Where to find out more

The Twenty Years' Crisis, 1919-1939
E. H. Carr

A Perfidious Distortion of History: The Versailles Peace Treaty and the success of the Nazis
Jürgen Tampke

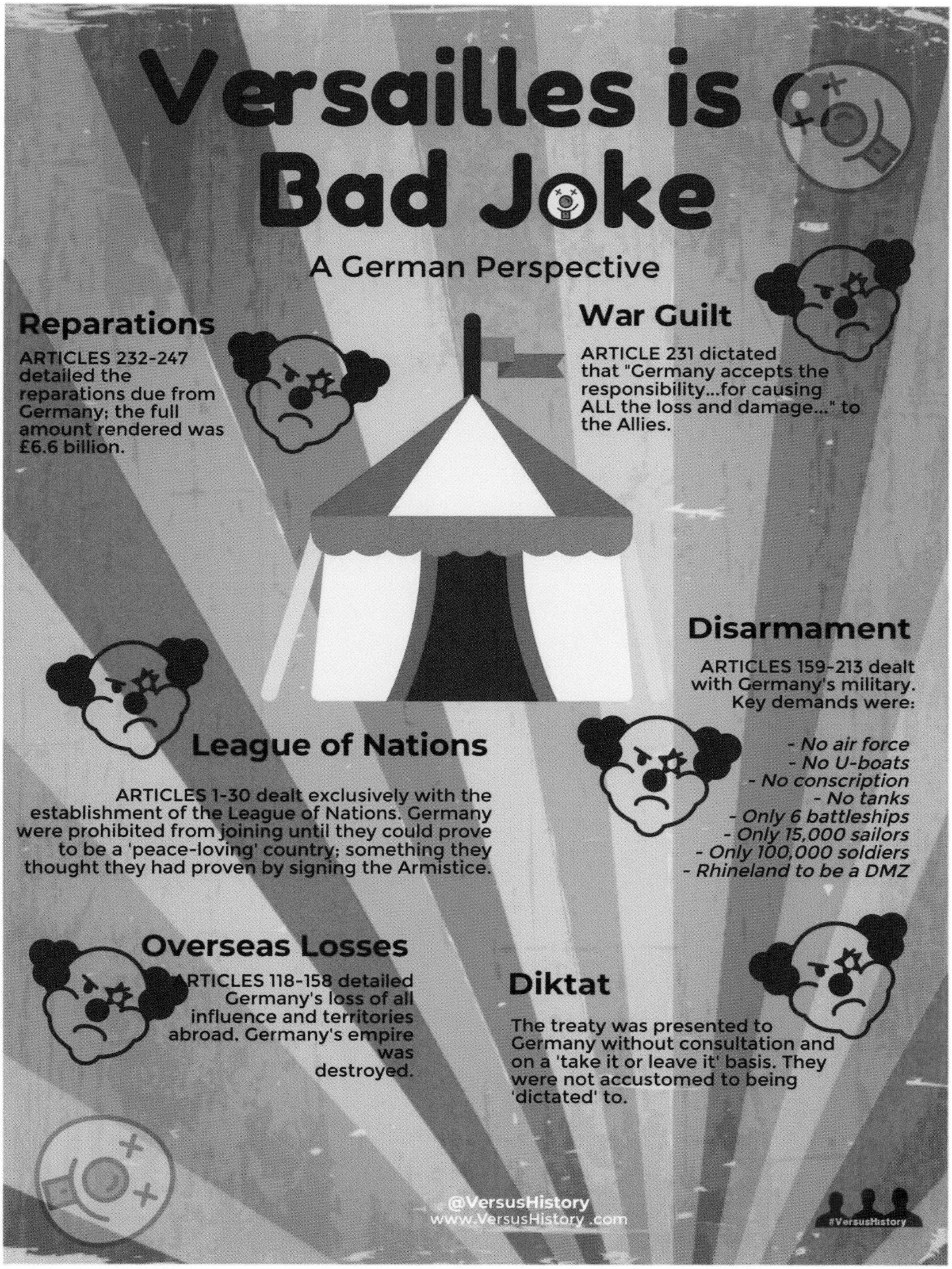
Versailles is Bad Joke
A German Perspective
Reparations
ARTICLES 232-247 detailed the reparations due from Germany; the full amount rendered was £6.6 billion.
War Guilt
ARTICLE 231 dictated that "Germany accepts the responsibility...for causing ALL the loss and damage..." to the Allies.
Disarmament
ARTICLES 159-213 dealt with Germany's military. Key demands were:
- No air force
- No U-boats
- No conscription
- No tanks
- Only 6 battleships
- Only 15,000 sailors
- Only 100,000 soldiers
- Rhineland to be a DMZ
League of Nations
ARTICLES 1-30 dealt exclusively with the establishment of the League of Nations. Germany were prohibited from joining until they could prove to be a 'peace-loving' country; something they thought they had proven by signing the Armistice.
Overseas Losses
ARTICLES 118-158 detailed Germany's loss of all influence and territories abroad. Germany's empire was destroyed.
Diktat
The treaty was presented to Germany without consultation and on a 'take it or leave it' basis. They were not accustomed to being 'dictated' to.
@VersusHistory
www.VersusHistory.com
#VersusHistory

In defence of Germany

Overview

In Articles 159-213 of the Treaty of Versailles, the fate of Germany's military was decided. As part of her punishment, Germany would have to significantly reduce her military, navy, and air force provisions. These military reductions were designed, primarily, to hinder the ability of Germany to wage another war – particularly one with France, whom she had attacked twice within fifty years.

Significance

One of the key motivations driving the terms of the Treaty of Versailles was punishment – the victorious Allies deemed, to varying degrees, that Germany must pay for the damage she had caused. However, there was more to the punishment than mere financial reparations. In the minds of Clemenceau and France, as part of their indemnity against future wars, and revenge for past ones, Germany deserved to be broken *and* humiliated. Consequently, for a country whose identity and history had been so entwined with her military strength, the reductions demanded by the treaty were devastating. More than this, they were emasculating – and purposefully so. The military potency of Germany was dissolved to the point where both external *and* internal threats could not be dealt with effectively. The violent political threats to early Weimar Germany would most certainly have been dealt with more decisively, but for the Versailles military clauses. To most Germans they represented a spiteful inclusion and would provide a 'war cry' for extremist parties looking to 'restore' Germany to her former glory. In addition, they felt cheated: disarmament was a key component of the discussions at Versailles – driven by Wilson's 14 Points – and yet Germany seemed to be the only country being held to account.

Historiography

"(The treaty was) ...extremely lenient in comparison with the peace terms that Germany herself, when she was expecting to win the war, had had in mind to impose on the Allies."

Correlli Barnett
The Collapse of British Power

Where to find out more

The Economic Consequences of the Peace
John Maynard Keynes

The Carthaginian Peace, or the Economic Consequences of Mr. Keynes
Étienne Mantoux

Versailles and Germany's Military
@VersusHistory
VersusHistory.com
The treaty took deliberate aim at Germany's military. France and Great Britain wanted to ensure that Germany could never again start a war. To this end, they radically reduced Germany's armed forces.
For a country with a proud military history, Versailles was the ultimate humiliation for Germany.
100,000 Soldiers
Reduced to only 2.2% of the German army that existed in 1918.
0 Planes
Germany used 97 different classes of aircraft during World War One.
6 Battleships
Right before the war ended, Germany had 19 battleships.
0 Tanks
Germany used 8 different classes of tank during World War One.
No Conscription
Germany used 13 million soldiers in the war. This would have been impossible without conscription.
15,000 Sailors
15,000 wasn't even half the number of sailors who died during World War One.

Papering over the cracks

Overview

Defeat in the First World War, and the concomitant overthrow of the Kaiser, unleashed a wave of violent unrest across Germany. The proclamation of a new German Republic, in the face of a Communist threat, on 9th November 1918 was just the beginning of the struggle to establish a new government. A National Assembly was formed as the result of elections in January 1919 and the following month they met in the quiet town of Weimar to begin the task of drawing up a Constitution for the nascent republic. The new Constitution was finally agreed on 31st July, but by that time there had been significant changes within Germany which would make the new Constitution difficult to uphold.

Significance

As the guiding document of the new German state, the Weimar Constitution had clear strengths. Universal suffrage for those aged 21 gave elected representatives legitimacy, while proportional representation ensured most Germans would have their views represented. By devolving some powers to regional governments and ensuring a balance of power between Reichstag, Chancellor and President, it seemed that autocracy was a thing of the past. However, upholding the Constitution would prove a challenge. Just one month before its introduction, the Weimar government had signed the notorious 'Diktat' at Versailles provoking the ire of nationalists who opposed the new republic. The divisions in Germany also made the system of proportional representation weak in practice. In the wake of elections in June 1920, Germany had four Chancellors in just three years, due to parliamentary arithmetic and national instability. A failure to effectively cope with adversity would plague the new government up until its dismantling by the Nazis.

Historiography

"In 1919, however, it was doubtful whether such a democratic constitution could work in the hands of a people that was neither psychologically nor historically prepared for self-government."

K Fischer
Nazi Germany. A New History

Where to find out more

The Weimar Republic 1919-33
Ruth Henig

Weimar Germany: Promise and Tragedy
Eric Weitz

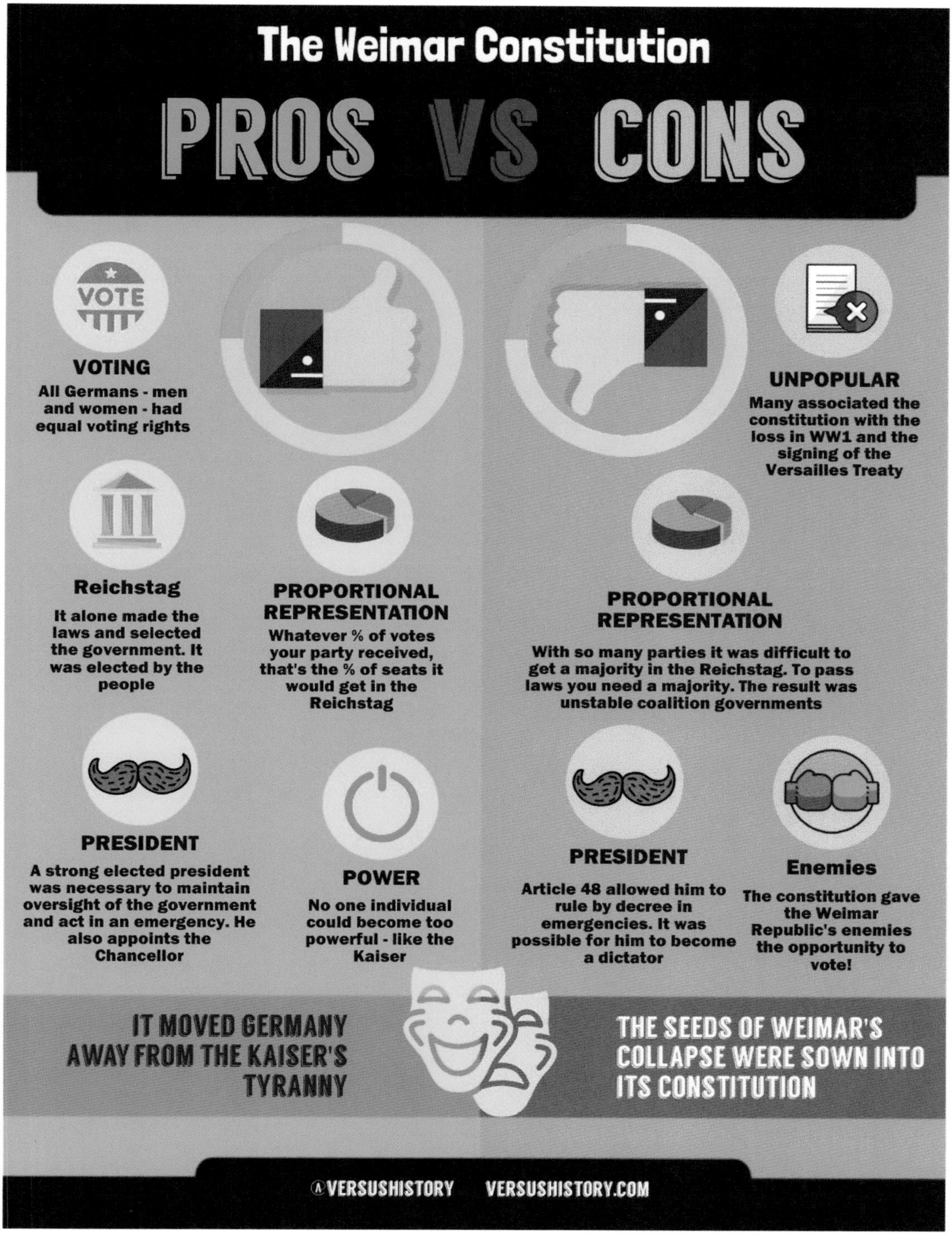
The Weimar Constitution
PROS VS CONS
VOTING
All Germans - men and women - had equal voting rights
VOTE
UNPOPULAR
Many associated the constitution with the loss in WW1 and the signing of the Versailles Treaty
Reichstag
It alone made the laws and selected the government. It was elected by the people
PROPORTIONAL REPRESENTATION
Whatever % of votes your party received, that's the % of seats it would get in the Reichstag
PROPORTIONAL REPRESENTATION
With so many parties it was difficult to get a majority in the Reichstag. To pass laws you need a majority. The result was unstable coalition governments
PRESIDENT
A strong elected president was necessary to maintain oversight of the government and act in an emergency. He also appoints the Chancellor
POWER
No one individual could become too powerful - like the Kaiser
PRESIDENT
Article 48 allowed him to rule by decree in emergencies. It was possible for him to become a dictator
Enemies
The constitution gave the Weimar Republic's enemies the opportunity to vote!
IT MOVED GERMANY AWAY FROM THE KAISER'S TYRANNY
THE SEEDS OF WEIMAR'S COLLAPSE WERE SOWN INTO ITS CONSTITUTION
@VERSUSHISTORY VERSUSHISTORY.COM

The gravity of the situation

Overview

1918-23 can be characterised as years of crisis, instability and suffering for Germany. The devastation caused by the war, coupled with the terms of Versailles, led to serious economic problems which the succession of short-lived governments failed to solve, culminating in hyperinflation in 1923. Germany was plagued by violent political uprisings from across the political spectrum; these groups fought each other, but also sought to gain power in a series of putsches, including Hitler's Beer Hall Putsch of 1923. A wave of 376 assassinations of predominantly left-leaning political figures merely added to the state of crisis. During this period, Germany's international standing was at its nadir. Excluded from the League of Nations, she was an international pariah, while her failure to pay her reparations led to French troops occupying the Ruhr region in 1921 and again in 1923.

Significance

The years 1918-23, while devastating for many, were not terminal for the new Weimar Republic. However, rather than its own strengths, it was the weakness of its opponents that allowed it to survive. The left-wing Communists and right-wing nationalists could just about be relied on to hate each other more than they did the government. Moreover, uprisings, such as that by the nascent Nazi Party in 1923, were often undermined by a lack of organization and decisiveness. The economic chaos of 1923, during which the value of the German mark fell so rapidly that prices could double within a day, saw the pinnacle of hardship for most Germans. The vulnerable were struck hardest; many of the elderly found the value of their pensions and savings virtually wiped out, while wage rises inevitably failed to keep up with the pace of inflation. The hardship, like the black hole opposite, sucked many Germans in and would not let them escape.

Historiography

"The fledgling republic was subjected not only to a hammering from abroad, but also to onslaughts from a variety of quarters at home… characterized by political violence, with frequent assassinations, coup attempts, strikes and demonstrations."

M. Fulbrook
A History of Germany 1918-2014

Where to find out more

The Last Winter of the Weimar Republic
Rüdiger Barth & Hauke Friedrichs

The Weimar Republic: The Crisis of Classical Modernity
Detlev Peuker

VersusHistory.com @VersusHistory
HYPERINFLATION
BANKRUPTCIES
INTERNATIONAL ISOLATION
TREATY OF VERSAILLES
FRENCH INVASION OF THE RUHR VALLEY
REPARATIONS
ATTEMPTED REVOLUTIONS
STAB IN THE BACK
POLITICAL ASSASSINATIONS
THE BLACK HOLE OF WEIMAR, 1918-23

Space invaders

Overview

On 11th January 1923 the 32nd French Infantry, at the command of the French Prime Minister Raymond Poincaré, marched across the German border and took up positions in the Ruhr. The previous year had seen Germany defaulting on reparation payments and, by the start of 1923, French patience had snapped. Once there, the French began to oversee the removal of raw materials and goods in lieu of the missing payments. The inhabitants of the Ruhr began a system of passive resistance but the French authorities circumvented this by bringing in French workers. International sympathy eventually turned against the French and at the London Conference of 1924, which established the Dawes Plan, it was agreed that the French would end their occupation of the Ruhr.

Significance

The occupation of the Ruhr by the French and Belgians had a crippling impact on Germany. The Ruhr was the industrial and manufacturing heartland of Germany. For a nation already struggling to pay reparations, the invasion was a disaster. It also reinforced Germany's impotence. Her army was only 100,000 strong and no match for the French, meaning that, in practical terms, there was little that the German military could do to remove the French. The route of passive resistance, encouraged by the German government's financial support of strikers, stoked the fire of the German far right's arguments that Weimar was doomed to failure and unable to stand up to international aggression. Finally, the occupation helped to usher in the most destructive crisis of the early years of Weimar. It exacerbated shortages of goods and caused the government to print money to finance the strikes. The occupation exacerbated the problems created by Versailles and led to a devastating period of hyperinflation, bringing Germany's economy to its knees.

Historiography

"The fiscal damage to the Reich and the states by the first six months of the Ruhr struggle was an estimated 827.6 million gold marks."

G. Feldman

The Great Disorder: Politics, Economics and Society in the German inflation, 1914-24

Where to find out more

The Ruhr Crisis1923-4
Conan Fischer

The Downfall of Money

'or

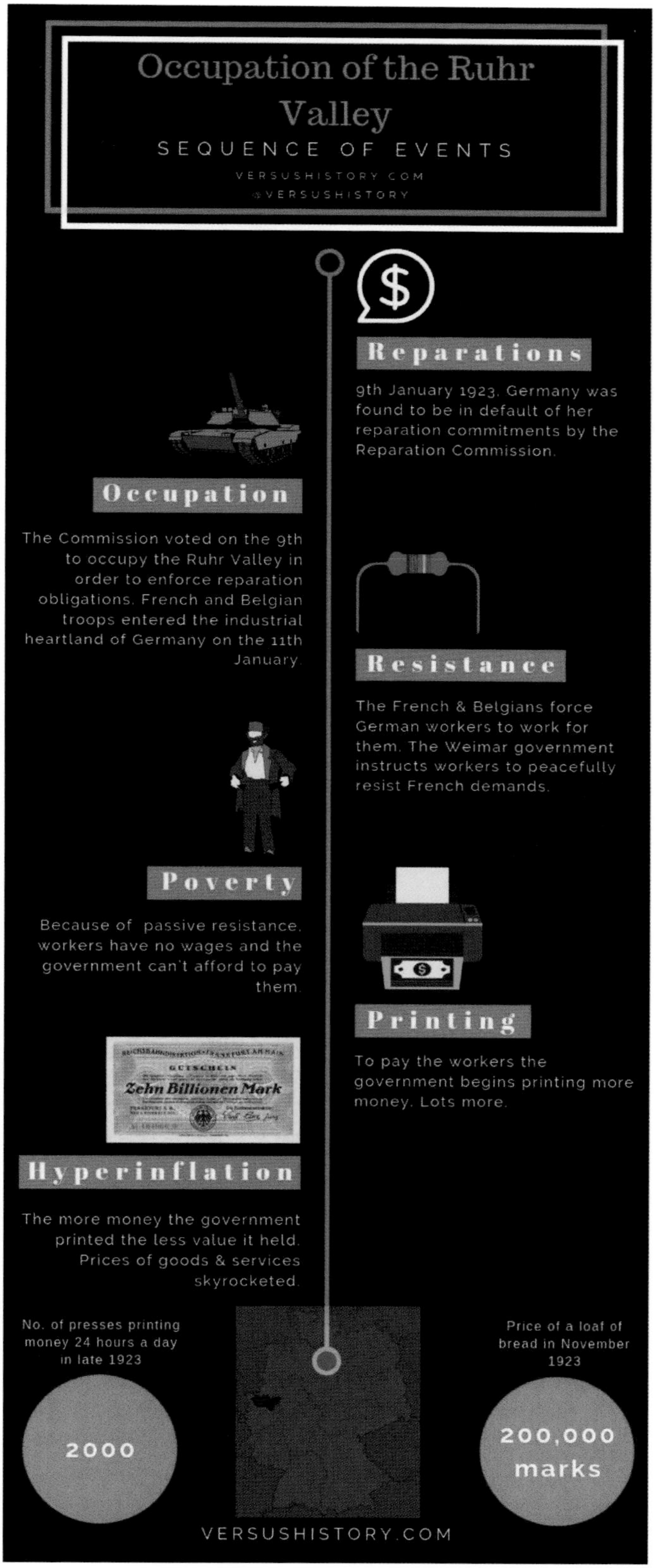
Occupation of the Ruhr Valley
SEQUENCE OF EVENTS
VERSUSHISTORY.COM
@VERSUSHISTORY
Reparations
9th January 1923. Germany was found to be in default of her reparation commitments by the Reparation Commission.
Occupation
The Commission voted on the 9th to occupy the Ruhr Valley in order to enforce reparation obligations. French and Belgian troops entered the industrial heartland of Germany on the 11th January.
Resistance
The French & Belgians force German workers to work for them. The Weimar government instructs workers to peacefully resist French demands.
Poverty
Because of passive resistance, workers have no wages and the government can't afford to pay them.
Printing
To pay the workers the government begins printing more money. Lots more.
GUTSCHEIN
Zehn Billionen Mark
Hyperinflation
The more money the government printed the less value it held. Prices of goods & services skyrocketed.
No. of presses printing money 24 hours a day in late 1923
2000
Price of a loaf of bread in November 1923
200,000 marks
VERSUSHISTORY.COM

Lessons in failure

Overview

On the night of 8th November 1923 the small, but growing, Nazi Party launched an audacious attempt to overthrow the government. With a force of 600 SA members, Hitler stormed into a meeting in a beer hall and announced a national revolution. Taking the President of Bavaria, Gustav von Kahr, and other influential figures hostage, he extracted promises of support and then, inexplicably, subordinates allowed them to go home. No longer under the control of the Nazis, the machinery of government swung into action. In Berlin, President Ebert declared a national emergency, while von Kahr and the heads of the police and army, von Seisser and von Lossow, organized a force to resist the Nazis in central Munich. With the veteran General Ludendorff by his side, Hitler pressed on. In the town centre there was a firefight and the putsch failed, leaving 16 Nazis and four policemen dead. The leaders of the Nazi Party were rounded up and arrested.

Significance

Though a disaster, in hindsight, the putsch was to prove a defining moment in the history of the Nazis. The trial put Hitler in the national consciousness, while the lenient sentences meant damage to the party was not terminal. Hitler's nine-month imprisonment allowed for a time of reflection. As well as writing Mein Kampf, the book that included the core elements of Nazi ideology, Hitler decided to adopt a new strategy, with populism, rather than armed revolution, seen as the route to power. The Nazi Party also exploited the putsch to create a mythology, with the 16 fallen being named "blood martyrs". After the Nazis came to power the putsch was memorialised such that it took on an almost supernatural significance. The putsch was a death of sorts for the Nazis, allowing it to be reborn with a different strategy, a clarified message, and a revered mythology.

Historiography

"…the sentence was… scandalous. No mention… of the four policemen shot by the putschists; the robbery of 14,605 billion paper marks was entirely played down…and the taking of a number of… city councillors as hostages were not blamed on Hitler."

Ian Kershaw
British Historians and the Treaty of Versailles

Where to find out more

The Trial of Adolf Hitler:The Beer Hall Putsch and the Rise of Nazi Germany
David King

A Guide to Hitler's Munich
David Mathieson

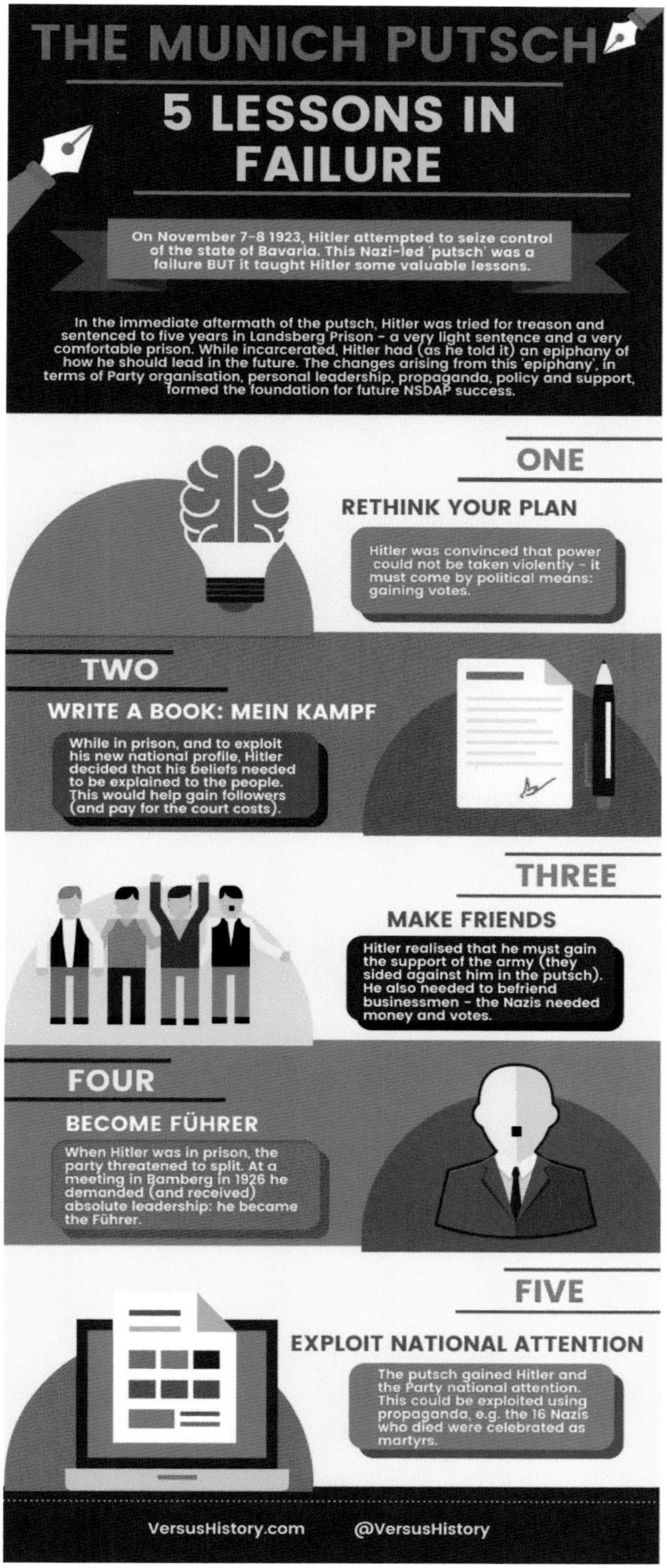
THE MUNICH PUTSCH
5 LESSONS IN FAILURE
On November 7-8 1923, Hitler attempted to seize control of the state of Bavaria. This Nazi-led 'putsch' was a failure BUT it taught Hitler some valuable lessons.
In the immediate aftermath of the putsch, Hitler was tried for treason and sentenced to five years in Landsberg Prison - a very light sentence and a very comfortable prison. While incarcerated, Hitler had (as he told it) an epiphany of how he should lead in the future. The changes arising from this 'epiphany', in terms of Party organisation, personal leadership, propaganda, policy and support, formed the foundation for future NSDAP success.
ONE
RETHINK YOUR PLAN
Hitler was convinced that power could not be taken violently - it must come by political means: gaining votes.
TWO
WRITE A BOOK: MEIN KAMPF
While in prison, and to exploit his new national profile, Hitler decided that his beliefs needed to be explained to the people. This would help gain followers (and pay for the court costs).
THREE
MAKE FRIENDS
Hitler realised that he must gain the support of the army (they sided against him in the putsch). He also needed to befriend businessmen - the Nazis needed money and votes.
FOUR
BECOME FÜHRER
When Hitler was in prison, the party threatened to split. At a meeting in Bamberg in 1926 he demanded (and received) absolute leadership: he became the Führer.
FIVE
EXPLOIT NATIONAL ATTENTION
The putsch gained Hitler and the Party national attention. This could be exploited using propaganda, e.g. the 16 Nazis who died were celebrated as martyrs.
VersusHistory.com
@VersusHistory

1923-29
relative stability

...cometh the Stresemann

Overview

Gustav Ernst Stresemann stood astride German politics for much of the 1920's. After a brief stint as chancellor in 1923, lasting only 102 days, he served as Germany's foreign minister for six years until his death of a stroke in October 1929. There were eight governments in this time, under three different chancellors and two presidents, yet Stresemann stayed in position. Despite his intense dislike of the Treaty of Versailles, Stresemann's pragmatism meant much of his effort was directed towards ensuring the Allies saw Germany as attempting to fulfill its obligations as a necessary route to ameliorating its effects. The years of his influence saw a degree of recovery from the earlier 'crisis years' of the Republic, and for many it was fitting that his coffin lay in state in the German Reichstag's chamber after his death.

Significance

Stresemann's impact in the 1920's was significant. Introducing a new temporary currency, the Rentenmark, in late 1923 solved the German hyperinflation crisis remarkably quickly, while his time as foreign minister helped Germany go from international pariah to partner. In foreign policy, Stresemann and Germany were dealt a terrible hand. Stresemann himself was frustrated that the Allied powers he negotiated with "...gave me nothing and the minor concessions they made always came too late", making his legacy more limited than he would have liked. Yet international agreements such as the Dawes Plan of 1924 and the Locarno Treaties were able, respectively, to reduce the annual reparations burden and guarantee peace with France. Germany's admission to the nascent League of Nations established Germany as a country, at least theoretically, on an equal footing with the Allies – a situation that would have been inconceivable without 'Weimar's greatest statesman'.

Historiography

"As he achieved one concession from the top of the list, two or three more were always added at the bottom. Stresemann gained most of his list, and no man in the Weimar Republic did more to destroy the Treaty of Versailles."

S. Marks
Illusion of Peace

Where to find out more

Gustav Stresemann: Weimar's Greatest Statesman
Jonathan Wright

Gustav Stresemann und die Republik
Deutsche Welle TV

Curriculum Vitae

GUSTAV STRESEMANN

SKILLS & EXPERIENCE

- Negotiating foreign treaties
- Economics Graduate
- Editor of magazines
- Chancellor, 1923 (102 days)
- Foreign Minister, 1924-29

HOBBIES

Popularised the wearing of a short lounge-suit jacket with morning dress attire

ACHIEVEMENTS

- Brought an end to the Ruhr Crisis of 1923
- Brought an end to hyperinflation and introduced a new currency: the Rentenmark
- Renegotiated reparations payments in the Dawes (1924) and Young (1929) Plans
- Reintegrated Germany into the international community with the Locarno and Kellogg-Briand Pacts
- Negotiated German membership of the League of Nations (1926)
- Negotiated a 25 billion mark loan from foreign businessmen (mostly US)
- Won the Nobel Peace Prize in 1926

CONTACTS

a: Weimar Germany
w: www.stability.com
e: gstresemann@weimar.com

My funeral...

VersusHistory.com @VersusHistory

Issues with expression

Overview

After the instability of the immediate postwar years, Weimar Germany witnessed, what some have termed, a 'Golden Age' in the Arts and Sciences. In almost every conceivable domain of creativity and empiricism, Germany saw remarkable and significant progress. In fact, between the years 1918-1933 there were eighteen German winners of Nobel Prizes in one discipline or another, including Gustav Stresemann himself in 1926. From the Bauhaus architectural movement started by Walter Gropius, to Bertolt Brecht's agitprop theatre, as well as Einstein's Theory of Relativity and Werner Heisenberg's work on quantum mechanics, Germany had rarely experienced such an explosion of cultural and scientific enlightenment. Of course, much of this progress and freedom came to a screeching halt when Hitler was appointed Chancellor of Germany.

Significance

One clear sign of prosperity in any country is the growth of artistic, cultural, and scientific domains that occur alongside it. Wealth generates investment, affords leisure time, and allows for expression and experimentation. It is no coincidence that when Gustav Stresemann helped restore a semblance of organisation and stability after the chaos of the years 1918-23, cultural creativity and scientific enterprise flared. Unfortunately, not everyone in Germany saw this burst of cultural change as valuable or even desirable. Many traditionalists saw these new trends of expressionism, *New Objectivity*, and abstraction as evidence of societal decay and degeneracy. Hitler was one of these who saw just that. When he came to power, state control over such expression would attempt to destroy it.

Historiography

"Remarkable for the way it emerged from a catastrophe, more remarkable for the way it vanished into a still greater catastrophe, the world of Weimar represents modernism in its most vivid manifestation."

Marcus Bullock
Review of the book *Weimar Surfaces* by Janet Ward

Where to find out more

Weimar Surfaces: Urban Visual Culture in 1920's Germany
Janet Ward

Women in the Metropolis
Katharina von Ankum (ed.)

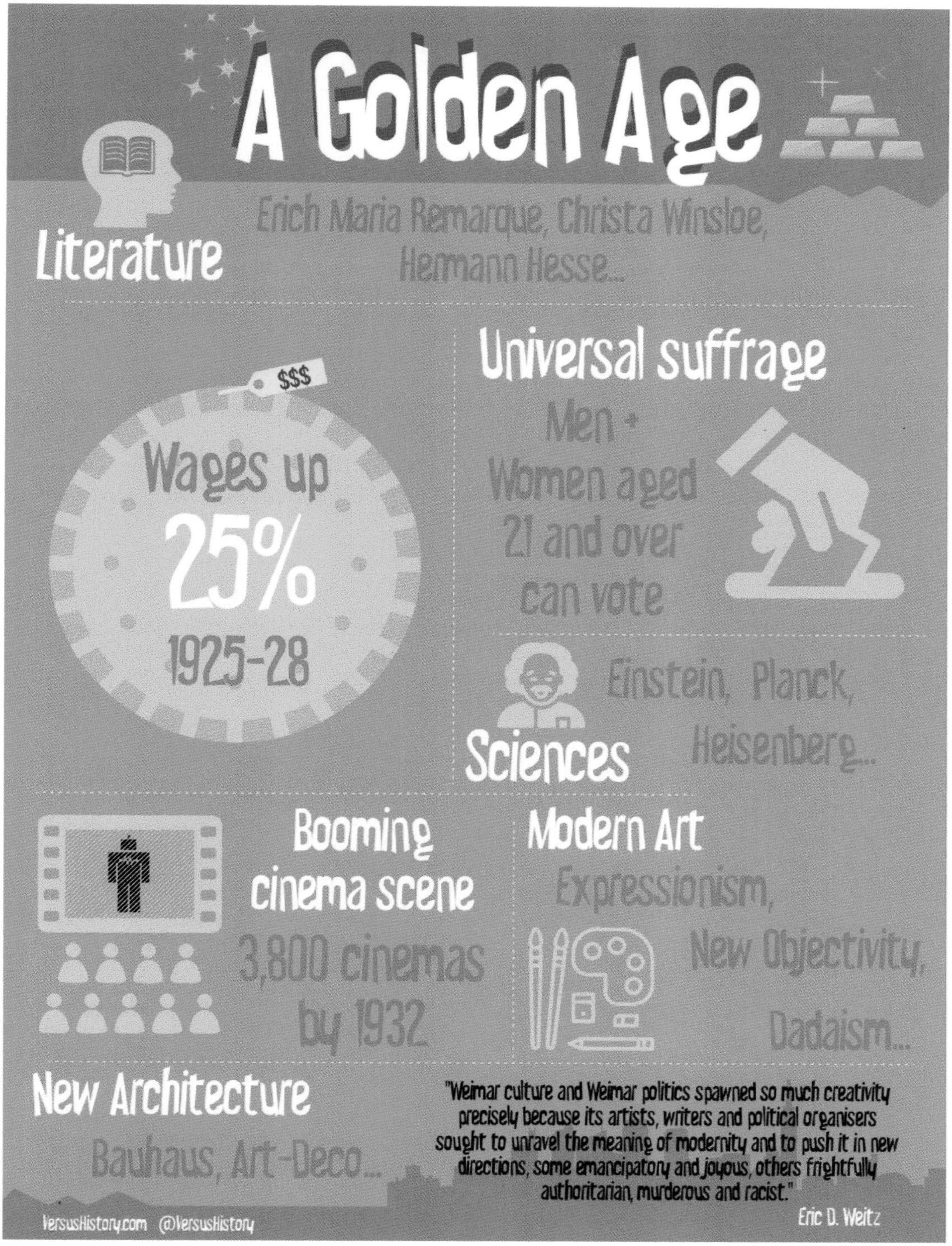
A Golden Age
Literature
Erich Maria Remarque, Christa Winsloe, Hermann Hesse...
$$$
Wages up
25%
1925-28
Universal suffrage
Men + Women aged 21 and over can vote
Einstein, Planck, Heisenberg...
Sciences
Booming cinema scene
3,800 cinemas by 1932
Modern Art
Expressionism,
New Objectivity,
Dadaism...
New Architecture
Bauhaus, Art-Deco...
"Weimar culture and Weimar politics spawned so much creativity precisely because its artists, writers and political organisers sought to unravel the meaning of modernity and to push it in new directions, some emancipatory and joyous, others frightfully authoritarian, murderous and racist."
Eric D. Weitz
VersusHistory.com @VersusHistory

Disco inferno

Overview

Some interpretations talk of the period 1924-29 as a 'Golden Age' in Germany, a time of jazz, cinema, cultural development and economic recovery. All of these did indeed exist to a degree, but the decade was also one of fragility. This was true economically, with Germany dependent on American loans and imports far outweighing exports, politically, with a string of short-lived coalition governments and socially, with a growing divide between traditional rural values and new, urban ones.

Significance

Stresemann's description of Germany as "dancing on a volcano" aptly describes how Germany's underlying problems were not solved in these years. New architectural movements like the Bauhaus school and the expansion of cinemas could not cover them up. The 'New Objectivity' (Neue Sachlichkeit) movement attempted to show the world as it really was through painting, and the picture was a grim one for many. Unemployment never dipped below 1 million, there were over 20 million working days lost to strikes and the cost of reparations as a proportion of Germany's Gross National Product more than doubled, placing a burden on the German people. Such a fragility manifested itself in the political sphere where the chancellorship moved back and forth as coalitions formed and crumbled. Moreover, the new President elected in 1925, Paul von Hindenburg, was known for his ultra-conservatism – having been nominated by the DNVP – and he had even asked the former Kaiser's son for permission to stand. Instability in Germany may have been dormant in the late 1920s, but disquiet was far from extinct.

Historiography

"The Roaring or Golden Twenties, saw a temporary return to domestic prosperity and a concurrent relaxation in international relations…(but) the political life of the republic still had not stabilized or matured. Between 1924 and 1929 governments were glued together by tenuous coalitions."

K. Fischer
Nazi Germany: A New History

Where to find out more

The Weimar Republic 1919-33
Ruth Henig

Weimar Germany: Promise and Tragedy
Eric Weitz

"Germany is in fact
dancing on a Volcano"
Gustav Stresemann, September 1929
The economy was built largely on foreign loans
1.4 million unemployed in 1928
Agriculture struggled in this decade due to low prices and farm debt
There were 15 chancellors in 15 years
There were 20 coalition governments in 14 years
30% of Reichstag election votes regularly went to opponents of Weimar
Hindenburg was elected President in 1925. He despised the Republic
Extremist parties like the Nazis gained large followings
VERSUSHISTORY.COM
@VersusHistory

A not-so-merry-go-round

Overview

The First World War, and particularly the reparations burden placed on Germany as a result, helped to bring about a new international financial order. In this system the European Allied powers of Britain and France owed huge debts to the USA but were themselves owed comparable levels of reparations from a defeated and economically suffering Germany. There was a recognition among the major powers by 1924 that facilitating this would require a kickstarting of the German economy via American loans, and from this was born the Dawes Plan of 1924. This plan laid the foundation of a system which allowed money to cycle and the economies of the powers to function, but also relied on the United States' burgeoning economy to underpin it.

Significance

Allowing such a cyclical system to function was crucial to each of the four powers involved, but for different reasons. The USA had little interest in obtaining reparations from Germany, but it was owed over $10 billion by the Allies. Meanwhile the Allies could not raise this money without the payment of significant reparations by Germany; the importance of which are illustrated by the invasion of the Ruhr after German defaults. Yet Germany's economy was clearly not fit to repay these on her own in 1923, requiring the USA to invest if there was not to be a litany of defaulting. As such, the enormous investment of American capital (some $25 billion between 1924-30) into Germany as part of, and following, the Dawes Plan, though generous, was also not as selfless as it may appear. Nor did most of this capital remain in Germany, with 60% flowing out again to Britain, France and Belgium in reparations. This was a cycle that allowed everyone to carry on, but it would only be able to last for as long as US capital flowed into Germany.

Historiography

"The Dawes Plan temporarily averted disaster... (but) created an unhealthy circulation of money. Germany borrowed money from the United States, gave that money to France and Britain, who in turn used it to pay back loans to the United States."

P. Payne

CRASH! How the Economic Boom and Bust of the 1920's Worked

Where to find out more

The Weimar Republic
John Hiden

The Economic Consequences of the Peace
John Maynard Keynes

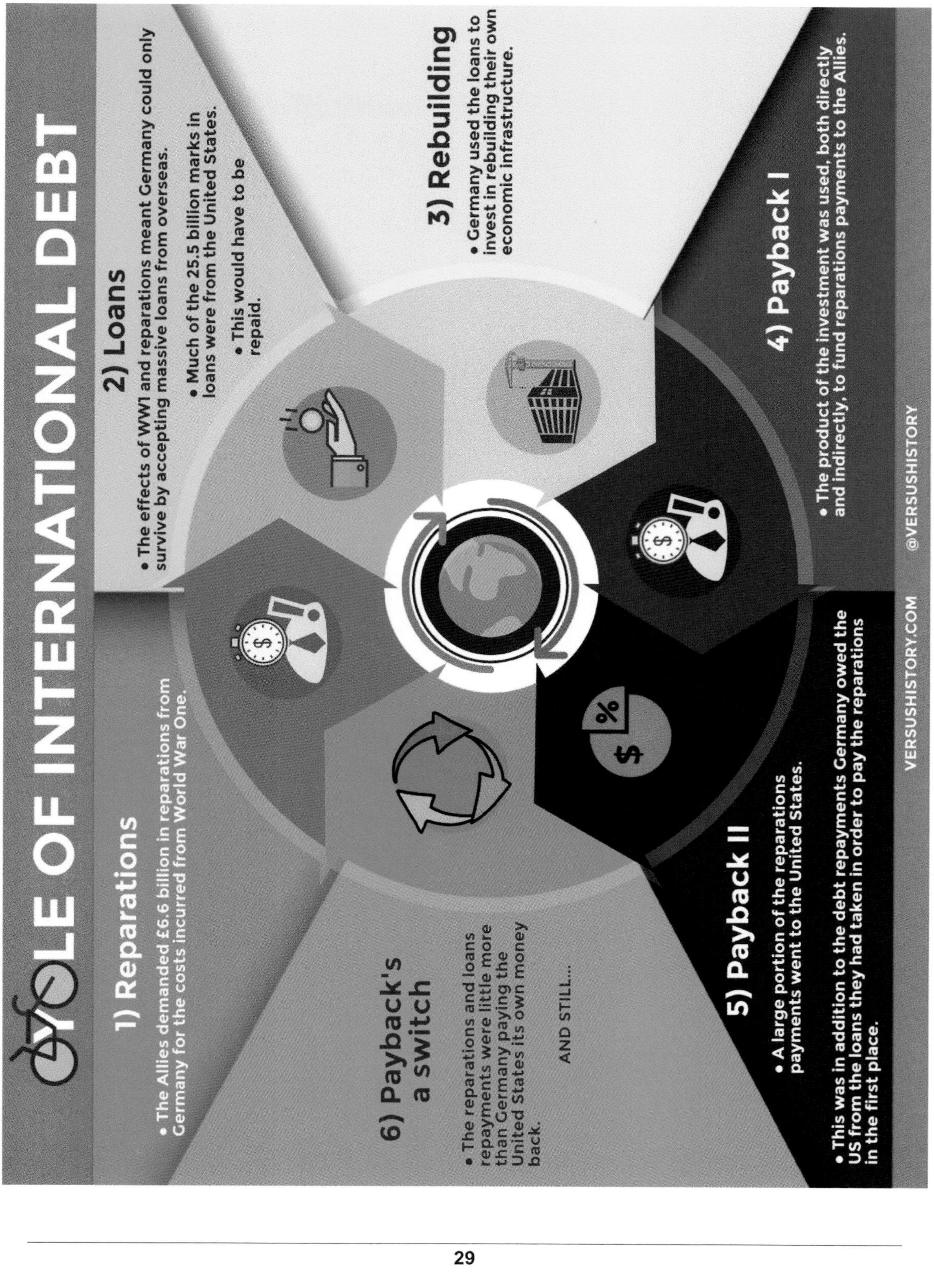
CYCLE OF INTERNATIONAL DEBT
1) Reparations
• The Allies demanded £6.6 billion in reparations from Germany for the costs incurred from World War One.
2) Loans
• The effects of WW1 and reparations meant Germany could only survive by accepting massive loans from overseas.
• Much of the 25.5 billion marks in loans were from the United States.
• This would have to be repaid.
3) Rebuilding
• Germany used the loans to invest in rebuilding their own economic infrastructure.
4) Payback I
• The product of the investment was used, both directly and indirectly, to fund reparations payments to the Allies.
5) Payback II
• A large portion of the reparations payments went to the United States.
• This was in addition to the debt repayments Germany owed the US from the loans they had taken in order to pay the reparations in the first place.
6) Payback's a switch
• The reparations and loans repayments were little more than Germany paying the United States its own money back.
AND STILL...
VERSUSHISTORY.COM
@VERSUSHISTORY

1929-33
Nazi support grows

A catalyst for catastrophe

Overview

The Great Depression the 1930's hit many nations across the world causing major suffering and hardship. Germany did not escape. Economically dependent on American loans, when these were recalled and the flow of capital dried up, German industry underwent a significant decline. Unemployment, never low in Weimar Germany, spiralled to a peak of 6 million, and industrial production declined by a third. Politically, the Depression heightened instability; extreme parties from both ends of the political spectrum grew in membership and influence. There were repeated elections which failed to bring stability and the Reichstag ceased to a be functioning legislative body.

Significance

The Great Depression of the 1930's was the catalyst for the end of the Weimar Republic. Already creaking politically, the system was unable to hold back a growing tide of extremist support. Millions of Germans were left jobless, homeless and without hope in the existing political system, leading to a growth in anti-Weimar parties. Within the Reichstag, Communist representation rose from 54 members in 1930, to 100 by November 1932, with the Nazis going from 107 to 196 in the same period. Hamstrung by these groups, the Reichstag proved unable to legislate, passing only five laws in 1932 and relying on the authoritarian measure of President Hindenburg passing laws by decree. It was in this situation of chaos that the leaders of Weimar felt driven to offer the chancellorship to the leader of the largest party in Germany, Adolf Hitler.

Historiography

"Of all the industrial states, Germany was undoubtedly the most vulnerable to a sudden downturn in economic conditions... The Depression dealt a devastating blow to democracy in Germany... (it) resorted increasingly to the use of Presidential decrees so that, by... May 1932, parliamentary democracy had virtually disappeared."

S.J. Lee
The European Dictatorships

Where to find out more

The Great Depression in Europe
Patricia Clavin

1931: Debt, Crisis and the rise of Hitler
Tobias Straumann

The Great Depression
Unemployment Rates in 1933
25%
10%
11%
30%
GERMANY
US INVESTMENT WORTH c'25.5 BILLION MARKS VANISHED ALMOST OVERNIGHT
NUMBER OF TIMES PRESIDENT HINDENBURG USED ARTICLE 48 IN 1932 ALONE: 60
DARMSTADTER UND NATIONALBANK - THE NATION'S SECOND LARGEST BANK - GOES BANKRUPT
1,000 million
WORTH OF GOLD AND FOREIGN EXCHANGE SENT OVERSEAS IN 2 WEEKS OF JUNE 1931
6 MILLION UNEMPLOYED IN 1933
55% THE FALL IN VALUE OF EXPORTS

A poisoned chalice

Overview

In theory the chancellor was intended to be the central decision maker in the Weimar Republic, just one who worked within significant democratic constraints. As head of government, he (being invariably male) appointed ministers and presided over their cabinet meetings, yet cabinet decisions were made by majority vote. A formulator of policy, the chancellor could help determine the legislative direction of the nation, yet all laws needed to be approved by the members of the Reichstag. This was made up of a kaleidoscope of parties from which the chancellor had to knit together a coalition; these groups could pass a vote of no confidence forcing him to resign. The chancellor was also to be dependent on the President for his position. Invited to become chancellor by the President, they could also be removed by him. There was even provision for the President to circumvent the chancellor, ruling by decree using Article 48, subject to Reichstag approval.

Significance

The checks and balances placed on the chancellor restricted his powers. However, it was the proportional voting system, and the increasingly weak coalitions the chancellor was required to preside over, particularly in the late Weimar Republic, that meant the role became virtually impotent by the early 1930s. In the face of the Depression, it is telling that legislative function increasingly migrated to the President rather than the chancellor. The very weakness of the position meant that in January 1933, President Hindenburg and the former chancellor Franz von Papen felt they could grant the chancellorship to Hitler. Instead of handing him Germany on a plate to do with as he wished, the experience of the previous ten years suggested they were passing him a poisoned chalice.

Historiography

"The expectation of the writers of the Constitution was that the chancellor, chosen by the President, would be the major leader of the German government and would direct domestic policy and foreign relations."

P. Bookbinder
Weimar Germany: The Republic of the Reasonable

Where to find out more

The Rise and Fall of Weimar Democracy
Hans Mommsen

The Weimar Republic Sourcebook
Anton Kaes, Martin Jay and Edward Dimenburg (eds.)

Weimar Germany's NINE chancellors in ten years. 1923-1933

(Nine indicates political instability)

CHANCELLOR

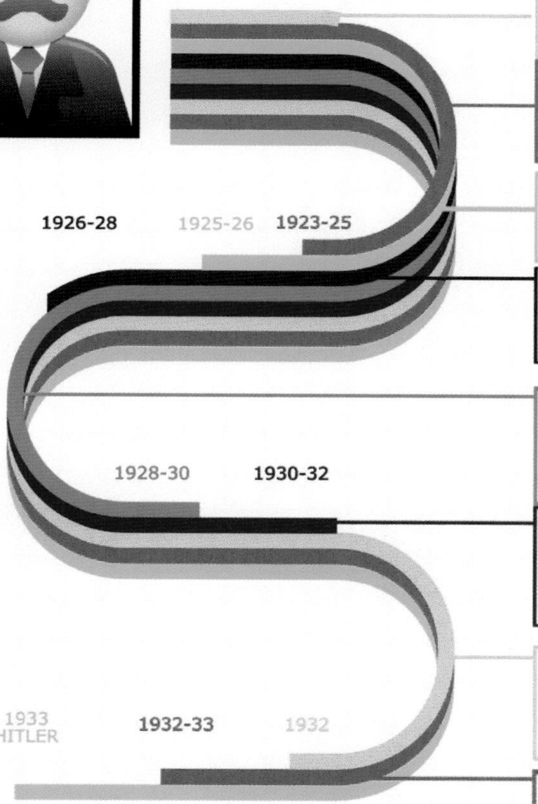

GUSTAV STRESEMANN
PARTY: German People's Party
DURATION: 109 DAYS

WILHELM MARX
PARTY: Centre Party
DURATION: 1 YEAR 46 DAYS

HANS LUTHER
PARTY: None
DURATION: 1 YEAR 117 DAYS

WILHELM MARX
PARTY: Centre Party
DURATION: 2 YEARS 26 DAYS

HERMANN MÜLLER
PARTY: Social Democratic Party of Germany
DURATION: 1 YEAR 272 DAYS

HEINRICH BRÜNING
PARTY: Centre Party
DURATION: 2 YEARS 61 DAYS

FRANZ VON PAPEN
PARTY: None
DURATION: 169 DAYS

KURT VON SCHLEICHER
PARTY: None
DURATION: 56 DAYS

www.VersusHistory.com
@VersusHistory

Extremely mainstream

Overview

The years 1929-33 were ones of extraordinary growth for the Nazi Party. A minor, extremist, regional party in 1928 underwent a transformation in fortunes to become the largest in the Reichstag by July 1932 and its leader, Hitler, coming second in Presidential elections in the same year. Professing to provide a solution to the hardship of the Depression, as trumpeted by the Nazi propaganda machine, their vote share increased. The spectacular growth was manifested in more than just electoral success. The paramilitary wing of the party, known as the SA, grew to number almost 2 million. Party membership enjoyed similar growth, while the growing number of endorsements and increased financial support from industrialists gave the party a financial basis from which to spread its message to the German population.

Significance

The growth of the Nazi Party was a necessary prerequisite to Hitler's appointment as Chancellor and his consolidation thereafter. Yet, popularity in itself would not bring power. Instead, Nazi growth is equally important for exposing the desperation and helplessness that the German people were feeling in the throes of the Depression. Nazi propaganda promised the German people *Arbeit* und *Brot* (Work and Bread), in stark contrast to Chancellor Brüning's austerity measures which had gained him the nickname of the 'Hunger Chancellor'. The desire for the seemingly simple solution promised by the Nazis seems to have been, for many, enough to outweigh the distasteful, racist and extremist elements of Nazi ideology and propel the Nazis to pre-eminence in German politics.

Historiography

(Talking of December 1932) "After an ascent of unparalleled swiftness the NSDAP had reached the limits of its electoral potential and now faced almost certain decline. The policy of legality, of mass mobilization for electoral campaigning had reached a dead end."

T. Childers
The Formation of the Nazi Constituency

Where to find out more

Hitler: Ascent, 1889-1939
Volker Ullrich

HistoryHit with Frank McDonough: The Rise of Hitler
HistoryHitTv

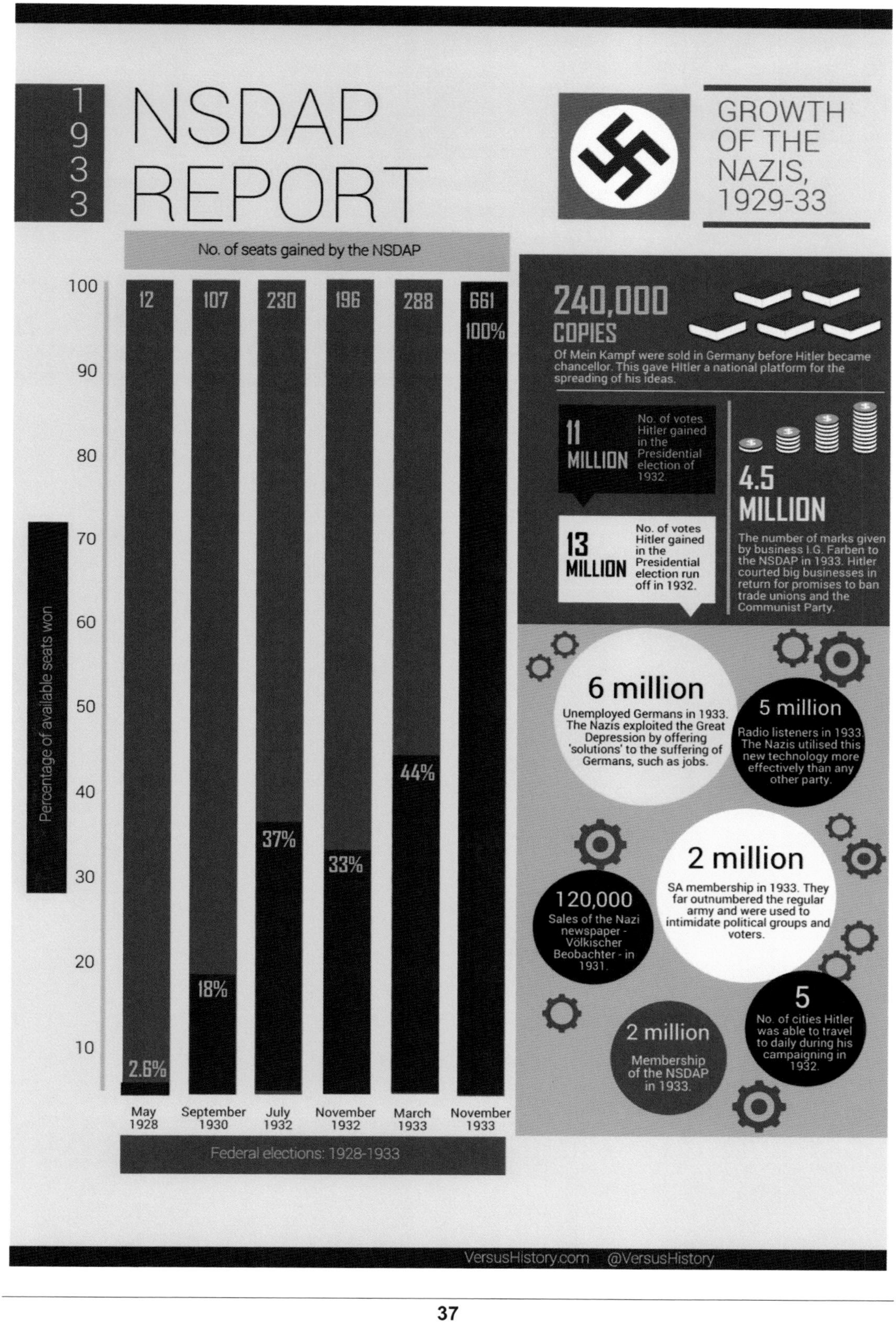
1933
NSDAP REPORT
No. of seats gained by the NSDAP
100
90
80
70
60
50
40
30
20
10
Percentage of available seats won
12
2.6%
107
18%
230
37%
196
33%
288
44%
661
100%
May 1928
September 1930
July 1932
November 1932
March 1933
November 1933
Federal elections: 1928-1933
GROWTH OF THE NAZIS, 1929-33
240,000 COPIES
Of Mein Kampf were sold in Germany before Hitler became chancellor. This gave Hitler a national platform for the spreading of his ideas.
11 MILLION
No. of votes Hitler gained in the Presidential election of 1932.
13 MILLION
No. of votes Hitler gained in the Presidential election run off in 1932.
4.5 MILLION
The number of marks given by business I.G. Farben to the NSDAP in 1933. Hitler courted big businesses in return for promises to ban trade unions and the Communist Party.
6 million
Unemployed Germans in 1933. The Nazis exploited the Great Depression by offering 'solutions' to the suffering of Germans, such as jobs.
5 million
Radio listeners in 1933. The Nazis utilised this new technology more effectively than any other party.
2 million
SA membership in 1933. They far outnumbered the regular army and were used to intimidate political groups and voters.
120,000
Sales of the Nazi newspaper - Völkischer Beobachter - in 1931.
5
No. of cities Hitler was able to travel to daily during his campaigning in 1932.
2 million
Membership of the NSDAP in 1933.
VersusHistory.com @VersusHistory

Taking a chance(llor)

Overview

On January 30th, 1933, the President of Germany, Paul von Hindenburg, appointed Adolf Hitler of the Nazi Party as chancellor. This role gave Hitler the chance to try and form a coalition in the Reichstag and become the new head of government. The powers of the chancellorship were restricted by the Weimar Constitution, but Hitler was to use (and abuse) his new position in order to take totalitarian control of Germany and unpick the fabric of the Weimar Republic.

Significance

Rather than an inevitability, it was a confluence of the Great Depression and the accompanying popularity of the Nazi Party, with the unstable political situation of the winter of 1932-3, that saw Hitler become chancellor. Even after becoming the largest party in the elections of July 1932, President Hindenburg claimed that "in front of God, his conscience and his country he could not justify giving the entire power of government to a single party…so hostile towards people who thought differently". Being leader of the largest party undoubtedly made Hitler a big player in the political machinations and calculations of the others at the top, yet the Nazis could for a while be ignored. They were forced to sit back and wait for six months and another election, as well as two new chancellors – von Papen and von Schleicher – to fail at holding coalitions together, before Hindenburg would be forced to rethink. At the urging of the scheming von Papen, and with all other avenues seemingly exhausted, Hindenburg was desperate enough to offer Hitler the chancellorship.

Historiography

"Out of a labyrinth of power struggles, Hitler emerged the victor. Few of the non-Nazi power brokers…had Hitler down as their first choice. But by January 1933, with other options apparently exhausted, most…were prepared to entertain a Hitler government."

I. Kershaw
Hitler: A Profile in Power

Where to find out more

The Death of Democracy: Hitler's Rise to Power and the Downfall of the Weimar Republic
Benjamin Carter Hett

The Rise of the Nazis Episode 1: Politics
BBC, 2019

HOW HITLER BECAME CHANCELLOR IN 1933

1 Effects of the Great Depression

During the Great Depression the Weimar government raised taxes, cut wages and reduced unemployment benefit. Wildly unpopular policies led many to vote for the Nazis, who promised work and food.

2 Popular Support

Successful electioneering led to the NSDAP increasing their number of seats in the Reichstag from 12 in 1928 to 230 in 1932. Hitler also ran for President and amassed 13 million votes in 1932.

3 Use of propaganda and violence

During 1929-32, two things happened: propaganda went into overdrive - to the point where Goebbels recorded his speeches and played them to audiences in his absence - and the violence of the SA escalated dramatically. The SA were even banned in 1932.

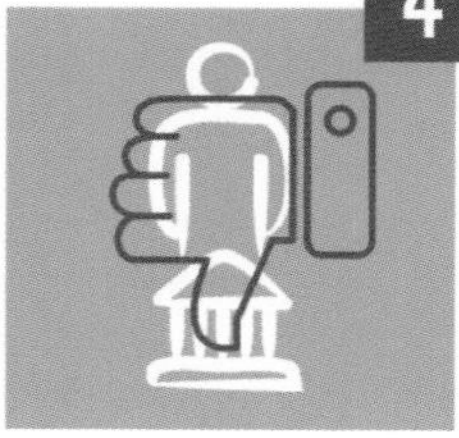

4 Ineffective Chancellors and scheming politicians

Successive Chancellors were unable to command a majority in the Reichstag and thus could not govern effectively. Brüning, von Papen and von Schleicher (Chancellors 1930-32) conspired against one another to the point of farce.

5 He was given the Chancellorship

Ultimately, President Hindenburg had little option but to appoint Hitler as Chancellor of Germany: he was the leader of the largest party in the Reichstag and all before him had failed.

All of these contributing factors were grounded in Hitler's abilities as an orator and his charismatic, forceful leadership.

"He learned how to become a charismatic speaker, and people, for whatever reason, became enamored with him..."
Prof. Bruce Loebs.

#VersusHistory

www.VersusHistory.com @VersusHistory

1933-34
Hitler's consolidation

Building a dictatorship

Overview

When Hitler became chancellor on January 30th, 1933, he was far from the unquestioned, all powerful leader of Germany he would become. Part of the reason for his appointment was in fact the perceived weakness of his position. In the most recent election of November 1932 the Nazis had actually lost support, claiming 34 fewer seats than they won in June. The seeming decline of Nazi support led many in the conservative establishment to think that Hitler could be controlled and manipulated, with constraints on his power enough to render him little more than a bit-part figure. Indeed, Hitler's Vice Chancellor, Franz von Papen of the Centre Party, claimed "…within two months we'll have pushed Hitler so far into the corner that he will squeak".

Significance

Appointing Hitler to the chancellorship can be argued as one of the gravest errors of judgement in history. However, the rationale that Hitler would not be able to act on his own to strengthen his position was actually borne out by events. Without a majority in the Reichstag and the cabinet, he could be outvoted. In February 1933 Hitler was indeed unable to fulfill his own legislative programme, as evidenced by the fact he asked President Hindenburg to dissolve the Reichstag and call new elections for March in the hopes of gaining a majority. When this failed, his attempts to consolidate power still required the co-operation, or at least acquiescence, of others. Surprisingly, this was forthcoming. The passage of the Reichstag Fire Decree was approved by Hindenburg, while it was the votes of the Centre Party that allowed the Enabling Act to pass through the Reichstag. The decision, or indecision, of others was at least as crucial as Hitler's own actions in allowing him to overcome the chancellorship's limitations.

Historiography

"To almost all seasoned observers, Hitler's political position on January 30 looked weak. It was designed to be weak…he had been put into office by a small circle of powerful men…they assumed they had Hitler squarely under control. Why should they not?"

B. Carter-Hett
The Death of Democracy

Where to find out more

The Coming of the Third Reich
Richard Evans

The Rise and Fall of Weimar Democracy
Hans Mommsen

CONSOLIDATE THIS

In January 1933, Hitler was given the Chancellorship, but both he and the Nazi Party were in positions of relative weakness. If Hitler was to achieve his goals, this position would have to be consolidated.

3 OUT OF 11

In Hitler's first Cabinet, there were only 3 Nazis: Hitler, Wilhelm Frick, and Hermann Goering. While the other members were mostly righ wingers, Hitler had no desire to rule in a coalition cabinet.

President

Hindenburg could remove Hitler at any point.

Reichstag

51%

In order to pass laws in the Reichstag, the Nazis needed a majority of seats. They didn't have this.

196

-34

In the November 1932 federal elections, the Nazis actually lost 34 seats in the Reichstag.

100

+11

In the same election, the Communist Party - the Nazis' arch enemy - gained 11 votes, becoming the 3rd largest party.

20-1

2 million

The SA outnumbered the army 20-1. Hitler needed the support of the army. He wouldn't get it as long as the SA existed in such numbers.

Hitler would overcome these obstacles:

- Because of his own actions.
- Because of the actions of others.
- Because of the environment at the time.

WWW.VERSUSHISTORY.COM @VERSUSHISTORY

CFEETLANDO

Overview

The eighteen months during which Hitler went from chancellor to dictator were marked by a series of events which increased his power and that of the Nazi Party. There are, however, a number of distinct phases that, with hindsight, can be identified. In the months immediately after becoming chancellor, there was a consolidation of Hitler's power over the government and decision-making in Germany, completed with the passage of the Enabling Act. Next, there was a raft of legislation limiting opposition, whether in the form of political parties, trade unions or regional governments. Thirdly, with the Night of the Long Knives, Hitler dealt with opposition within the Nazi Party. Finally, the death of President Hindenburg and the oath of allegiance from the army removed any constitutional and military obstacles.

Significance

The key question for historians is whether Hitler arrived in his unassailable position in 1934 due to a clear, planned and orchestrated set of policies or whether this was a more haphazard, opportunistic chain of events. The truth, however, is most likely to be found somewhere in the middle of these extremes. Hitler was clearly an opportunist; chance events like the Reichstag Fire and Hindenburg's death required swift, decisive action for political gains to be made, while the Night of the Long Knives showcased Hitler's ability to implement and then get away with actions far beyond the pale. Yet, Hitler's actions in other areas, such as the Enabling Act and his, admittedly short-lived, alliance with the Catholic Church reveal perhaps a medium-term strategy behind his actions. Whatever the strategy, these events had far-reaching ramifications for Germany and beyond.

Historiography

"The rapid progress of events which began with Hitler's appointment and ended on 2 August 1934 with the union of offices of president and chancellor…(were) a seizure of complete power. In quick succession, Hitler…implemented radical policies…thus turning democracy into dictatorship."

C. Leitz
The Third Reich

Where to find out more

Hitler 1889-1936: Hubris
Ian Kershaw

In Our Time: Hitler in History
BBC Radio 4 Archive

HITLER'S CONSOLIDATION OF POWER, 1933-34

'CFEETLANDO'

C

HITLER BECOMES CHANCELLOR, 30TH JANUARY 1933

Hitler is invited to become chancellor of Germany by President Hindenburg. His immediate position is one of weakness. He must consolidate power in order to become 'Führer'.

F

FIRE IN THE REICHSTAG BUILDING, 27TH FEBRUARY, 1933

Hitler exploits the fire to claim that the Communists are planning a revolution. An emergancy decree is passed the next day: *For the Protection of the People and the State.* This suspends freedoms of speech, the press, of assembly and removes restraints on police investigations.

E

ELECTION, 5TH MARCH, 1933

Through a campaign of violence, intimidation and suppression, the Nazis polled 43.91% of the votes. Still not a majority but...

E

THE ENABLING LAW PASSED 23RD MARCH, 1933

Hitler used the Reichstag Fired Decree to prevent the KDP from taking part in the vote and, using a coalition with the Catholic Centre Party, passed a law which enabled him to govern without the consent of the Reichstag. Germany effectively became a dictatorship from this point onwards.

T

TRADE UNIONS REPLACED, 2ND MAY, 1933

Hitler replaced all trade unions with the German Labour Front. This gave him control over national industries and their workers - who had traditionally voted for either the KDP or the SDP. Strike became illegal and the Nazis controlled wages and working hours.

LA

LAW AGAINST THE FORMATION OF NEW PARTIES, 14TH JULY, 1933

Hitler passed this law which effectively banned all other political entities. Germany became a one party state.

N

NIGHT OF THE LONG KNIVES, 30TH JUNE-2ND JULY, 1934

Ernst Röhm, along with other SA leaders and political threats, were arrested and executed in this purge which removed opposition to Hitler and regained the support of the army.

D

DEATH OF HINDENBURG, 2ND AUGUST, 1934

The President of Germany - Hitler's only real obstacle to absolute power - died. Hitler backdates a law to August 1st which allows him to combine the office of the Presidency with that of the Chancellor. He is now the Führer of Germany.

O

ARMY *'OATH TO THE LEADER'*, 30TH AUGUST, 1934

Hitler gained the loyalty of the military through this forced oath of allegiance.

A burning issue

Overview

Just after 9pm on the evening of February 27th, 1933, the German parliament building – the Reichstag – was set on fire and largely destroyed. A young Dutch communist, Marinus van der Lubbe, was found on the scene by police and arrested. Rumors abounded that this was the beginning of a communist conspiracy and the signal for a large-scale uprising against the government. Put on trial later in the year, along with four communist leaders who were acquitted, van der Lubbe was found guilty and executed in January 1934.

Significance

It was a combination of the timing of the fire and its exploitation by Hitler that made it arguably the pivotal moment in the rise of the Nazis. Elections were due to be held just one week later, on March 5th, and it was in this context that Hitler persuaded President Hindenburg that a restriction on civil liberties was needed. The Reichstag fire created a sense that Germany was under attack, providing justification for an emergency decree. This decree was enforced by the police (overseen since January by Hermann Göring) and led to the locking up of thousands of KPD members – including their leader Ernst Thalmann – as well as the banning of communist publications, just before the election. In addition, murders and political violence carried out by Nazi stormtroopers were allowed to escape police action. Crucially, after the elections the decree stayed in force. Hitler would use it to ban communist members from taking up their seats in the Reichstag, but it would also be the legal basis for repression of opposition from many other quarters.

Historiography

"The Reichstag Fire Decree was one of the pivotal steps the Nazis took toward the establishment of a single party state…thousands of Hitler's Decrees were based explicitly on it…the Reichstag Fire Decree was never abolished during the Nazi period; thus, for the next 12 years Hitler ruled under what amounted to Martial Law."

M.Head
Emergency Powers in Theory and Practice: The Long Shadow of Carl Schmitt

Where to find out more

Burning the Reichstag: An Investigation into the Third Reich's Enduring Mystery
Benjamin Carter Hett

Hitler: Ascent, 1889-1939
Volker Ullrich

FIRE IN THE REICHSTAG

How Hitler exploited the fire to consolidate his authority

27th February 1933

Exactly 4 weeks after Hitler became Chancellor, the seat of Germany's parliament was set on fire. A Dutch communist named Marinus van der Lubbe was named by Hitler's government as the culprit.

"If this fire, as I believe, is the work of the Communists, then we must crush out this murderous pest with an iron fist."
Hitler

THE REICHSTAG FIRE DECREE

The next day, Hitler persuaded President Hindenburg to use ARTICLE 48 to issue a decree which withdrew many civil liberties guaranteed by the Weimar Constitution. The decree gave Hitler the tools to remove his political opponents and centralise his power.

28th February

4000

The approximate number of arrests made on the night of the decree. Most of these were members of the Communist Party (KPD).

March 1933

+92

The increase in number of seats gained by the NSDAP in the March election. This was partly as a result of the anti-communist measures employed after the fire.

FREE SPEECH ABOLISHED

Along with free assembly, the right to privacy, and freedom of the press.

This allowed Hitler to ban any publication, meeting, speech, and radio station that was not 'friendly' to the NSDAP.

HABEAS CORPUS

All prisoners in Germany had the right to be brought before a court in order to establish whether their incarceration was legal. This age-old recourse was abolished.

The Nazis could now detain whomever they chose without having to justify in a court why they had done so. In this way, the Nazis were able to round up any opponents they so chose.

BANNED THE KPD

The Communist Party was not banned immediately (this happened on the 14 July) but being a member became synonymous with treason.

The day after the election of March 5, all 81 of those KPD members who had gained seats in the Reichstag were detained. This left 81 empty seats that could not vote against the NSDAP.

ENABLING ACT

On 23rd March, Hitler convinced the members of the Reichstag (now meeting in the Kroll Opera House) to vote in favour of this act.

The act gave him the power to enact laws without their consent. Because of the above, there were insufficient KPD members who could vote against it.

ONLY 7.8% OF PEOPLE VOTED AGAINST THE NSDAP IN THE NEXT ELECTION

www.VersusHistory.com @VersusHistory

Enabling a dictator

Overview

The *Law to Remedy the Distress of the People and the Reich* passed through the Reichstag on March 23rd 1933, ostensibly allowing Hitler to solve Germany's economic problems. Its passage was accompanied by some controversy; the 81 Communist deputies had been banned from taking up their seats and there was intimidation of the remaining deputies. Yet it was, strictly speaking, legal. The Act stated that, for the next four years, laws could be created by the German government, that is the Cabinet and Chancellor, without the need for approval by the Reichstag. It also stated that any laws passed did not need to stick to the constitution, so long as they did not affect the Reichstag or Reichsrat.

Significance

The Enabling Act was the legal foundation of much that the Nazi Party would go on to do in Germany. The need for compromise and coalition agreement in the Reichstag vanished. Parties that had helped enable Hitler, such as the Catholic Centre Party which supported the passage of the Act, would be banned through the *Law Against the Founding of New Parties*, passed using the provisions of the Enabling Act. Despite needing to be renewed after four years, this was nothing other than a formality. By April 1937 the Nazis had complete control of Germany and the Reichstag would rubber-stamp the renewal of the Act twice more. By removing the influence of the Reichstag, the Enabling Act effectively ended democracy and the Weimar Republic. Instead two men alone would each have the authority to legislate by decree: President Hindenburg and Chancellor Hitler. However, Hindenburg's authority to do so could be overturned by the Reichstag; there were no such checks on Hitler.

Historiography

"...after the passage of the Enabling Law and subsequent legislation, some of the Weimar organs of government either ceased to exist or became rubber stamps for Hitler's dictatorship...the Reichstag was impotent...and met only to hear speeches from Hitler."

R. Wolfson & J. Laver
Years of Change: 1890-1945

Where to find out more

The Coming of the Third Reich
Richard J. Evans

Versus History Podcast, Episode #17: Hitler: Chancellor to Fuhrer
Versus History

23rd March 1933

HITLER: ENABLED

VersusHistory.com @VersusHistory

5. The Reichstag voted itself out of existence, legislatively speaking.

4. Hitler's Reich Cabinet (in effect, Hitler himself) could pass laws without the Reichstag's consent.

3. Hitler consolidated with laws such as The Law Against the Formation of New Parties on July 14th 1933.

2. It allowed Hitler to create a one party dictatorship - led by himself.

1. HOWEVER, as long as Hindenburg was still President, Hitler would never truly be a dictator...

THE ENABLING LAW

On the 23rd March 1933, a law was passed by 83% of the Reichstag deputies - 444 voting in favour and 94 against - that would fundamentally alter the constitutional and legal framework of Germany.

The ***Law to Remedy the Distress of the People and the Reich*** was enacted by a Reichstag intimitidated by SA troops while missing all KPD, as well as 26 SPD, deputies.

Night moves

Overview

On the night of 29th June 1934, murder came to the sleepy lakeside spa town of Bad Wiessee. Many leaders of the SA were dragged from their beds and summarily executed. Significantly, these men included Ernst Röhm, the commander of the now millions strong Nazi paramilitary organisation. As well as removing the leadership of the SA in one fell swoop, Hitler used the Night of the Long Knives to settle old scores removing former party rivals such as Gregor Strasser and old opponents such as Kurt von Schleicher and Gustav von Kahr. Yet, despite having ordered murder, Hitler claimed that he acted on behalf of the nation in order to save the nation.

Significance

According to the 'official' Nazi version of events, the Night of the Long Knives was significant for having stopped a plot led by Ernst Röhm for a new revolution in Germany. However, it was most significant for both illustrating and establishing Hitler's unchecked power. Hitler took full responsibility in a speech to the Reichstag; yet, despite having carried out state sponsored murder he was able to get away without negative consequence. Indeed, the murders strengthened his power. As well as removing annoyances and a potential threat to his position in Röhm, Hitler's actions won him the support of the army and importantly its commanders delighted at the weakening of the numerically superior SA. Crucially the Night of the Long Knives showed that it was not the rule of law that would be of paramount importance in Germany. Instead, it was the will of one man, free to act as judge, jury and executioner, that would hold ultimate authority.

Historiography

"While international opinion condemned the state-sanctioned murders, labeling Hitler a common thug… in Germany popular sentiment was clearly with him. The general public celebrated him as a savior, liberating them from the plague of SA viciousness."

T. Childers
The Third Reich: A History of Nazi Germany

Where to find out more

Night of the Long Knives: Forty-Eight Hours That Changed the History of the World
Paul Maracin

Stormtroopers: A New History of Hitler's Brownshirts
Daniel Siemens

Rise of the Nazis Episode 3: The Night of the Long Knives
BBC, 2019

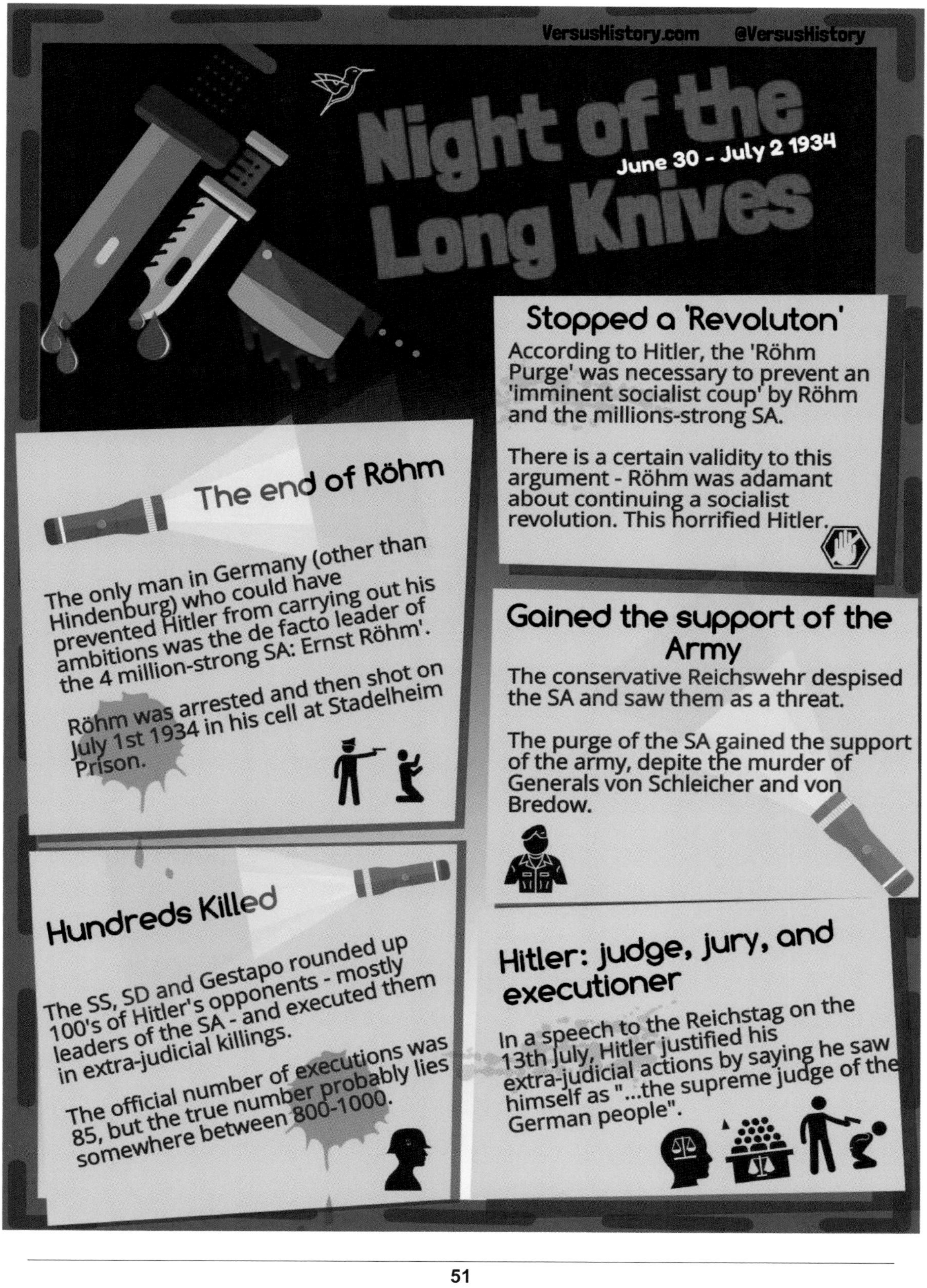
VersusHistory.com
@VersusHistory
Night of the Long Knives
June 30 - July 2 1934
Stopped a 'Revoluton'
According to Hitler, the 'Röhm Purge' was necessary to prevent an 'imminent socialist coup' by Röhm and the millions-strong SA.
There is a certain validity to this argument - Röhm was adamant about continuing a socialist revolution. This horrified Hitler.
The end of Röhm
The only man in Germany (other than Hindenburg) who could have prevented Hitler from carrying out his ambitions was the de facto leader of the 4 million-strong SA: Ernst Röhm'.
Röhm was arrested and then shot on July 1st 1934 in his cell at Stadelheim Prison.
Gained the support of the Army
The conservative Reichswehr despised the SA and saw them as a threat.
The purge of the SA gained the support of the army, depite the murder of Generals von Schleicher and von Bredow.
Hundreds Killed
The SS, SD and Gestapo rounded up 100's of Hitler's opponents - mostly leaders of the SA - and executed them in extra-judicial killings.
The official number of executions was 85, but the true number probably lies somewhere between 800-1000.
Hitler: judge, jury, and executioner
In a speech to the Reichstag on the 13th July, Hitler justified his extra-judicial actions by saying he saw himself as "...the supreme judge of the German people".

The missing piece of the jigsaw

Overview

Paul von Hindenburg was an unlikely candidate for President. In 1925 he did not even stand for election in the first round, only joining the race as a compromise candidate when conservative parties could not agree who to support. Similarly, in 1932 and at the age of 85, he had to be persuaded to stand for office again. Yet despite his reluctance, Hindenburg as President wielded significant powers: issuing decrees, appointing chancellors and dissolving governments. These powers were frequently used in the early 1930's and were retained by Hindenburg after Hitler's appointment, until his death from lung cancer on 2nd August 1934.

Significance

While Hindenburg was alive he, theoretically, had the power as President to remove Hitler, dissolve the Reichstag and call new elections. In practice, given both Hitler's support and Hindenburg's worsening condition, this was unlikely to be used. However, his death removed the last legal checks on Hitler's power. Characteristically, Hitler moved swiftly to ensure he gained from Hindenburg's demise. Having already instructed the Cabinet to pass the "Law Concerning the Head of State of the German Reich", which would combine the offices of President and Chancellor on Hindenburg's death, Hitler sought to legitimize this through a referendum on 19th August. With 88% support, and the army now swearing loyalty to him in person, Hitler could be confident that his position as Führer of Germany was unshakeable. Essentially, Hindenburg's death confirmed rather than created this security for Hitler but, as such, it presented him with the final piece of the consolidation jigsaw that he needed.

Historiography

"In the few weeks embracing the Röhm affair (Night of the Long Knives) and the death of Hindenburg, Hitler had removed all remaining threats to his position…He was now institutionally unchallengeable, backed by the 'big battalions', adored by much of the population. He had secured total power. The Führer state was established. Germany had bound itself to the dictatorship it had created."

I. Kershaw
Hitler: A Biography

Where to find out more

Hindenburg: Power, Myth and the Rise of the Nazis
Anna von der Goltz

The Coming of the Third Reich
Richard J. Evans

DEATH OF HINDENBURG

THE FINAL PIECE OF THE JIGSAW

When the 87 year old President of Germany - Paul von Hindenburg - died in the morning of the 2nd August 1934, the final obstacle to Hitler's dictatorship was removed. In anticipation of the death, Hitler had a law already crafted which would be backdated to the day before Hindenburg's death. Within hours of the President's death, this law came into effect, with profound consequences.

"I swear by God this sacred oath: I will render unconditional obedience to Adolf Hitler..." Oath of allegiance, German Army

HITLER COMBINED THE CHANCELLORSHIP WITH THE PRESIDENCY: **HE BECOMES FüHRER OF GERMANY.**

AS GERMANY'S FüHRER, HITLER WAS NOW **COMMANDER IN CHIEF OF THE ARMED FORCES.**

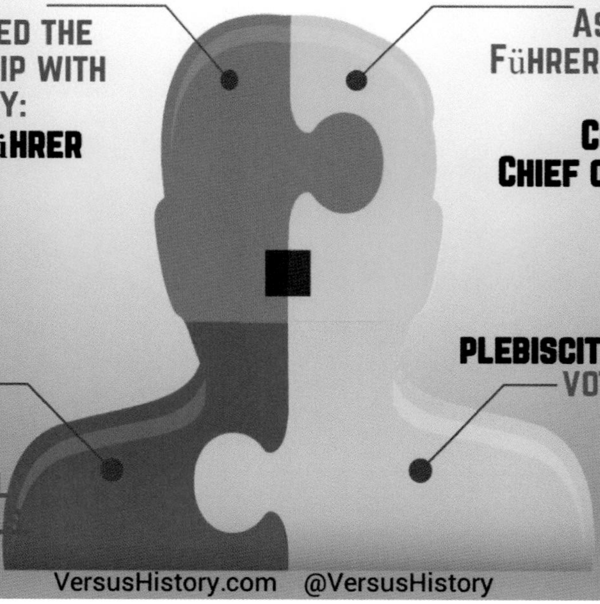

AN 'OATH OF LOYALTY' WAS TAKEN BY THE ARMED FORCES AND ALL PUBLIC OFFICIALS.

ON 19TH AUGUST, A **PLEBISCITE** WAS HELD TO VOTE ON HITLER'S ACTIONS. 88% VOTED IN FAVOUR.

VersusHistory.com @VersusHistory

1933-45
domestic policy

Razing to rebuild

Overview

The Nazi Party, and its forerunner the German Workers' Party, was founded in a period of turbulence and unrest. The years immediately after World War One saw uprisings, protests, street battles and the establishment of a new republic. It is within this context that National Socialist aims were first articulated in the 25-Point Programme. While there was internal Party debate about certain elements of this manifesto in the 1920's, there were other tenets about which all were unified. For example, the nature of the Party's socialism was often quarreled over, whereas the desire for a strong Germany, with the nation taking precedence over the individual, was to be an enduring aim throughout the Party's rise and governance.

Significance

Nazi aims for Germany were radical and would require, in some cases, a destruction of existing systems. National Socialism would then rebuild these systems so as to achieve their ideological aims. Versailles, often seen as the symbol and, in part, creator of German weakness, would have to be overturned. This, of course, would bring resistance from other powers. The establishment of a strong leader – a führer – would require breaking much of the political structure of Weimar Germany and the abandoning of parliamentary governance. The creation of a racially 'pure' German race supposedly required the purging of non 'Aryans' in order to create a new 'Peoples Community'. The transformative and inviolable nature of these aims would drive many Nazi actions, from the desperate power grab in the Munich Putsch of 1923 to the systematic dismantling of the political system during 1933-4, as well as the escalating persecution of Germans who did not fit Nazi ideals.

Historiography

"Among ordinary Party activists...the most important aspect of Nazi ideology was its emphasis on social solidarity - the concept of the organic racial community of all Germans - followed at some distance by extreme nationalism and the cult of Hitler."

Richard J. Evans
The Coming of the Third Reich

Where to find out more

Nazi Ideology Before 1933: A Documentation
Barbara Miller Lane and Leila J. Rupp

Nazism as Fascism: Violence, Ideology and the Ground of Consent in Germany 1930-45
Geoff Eley

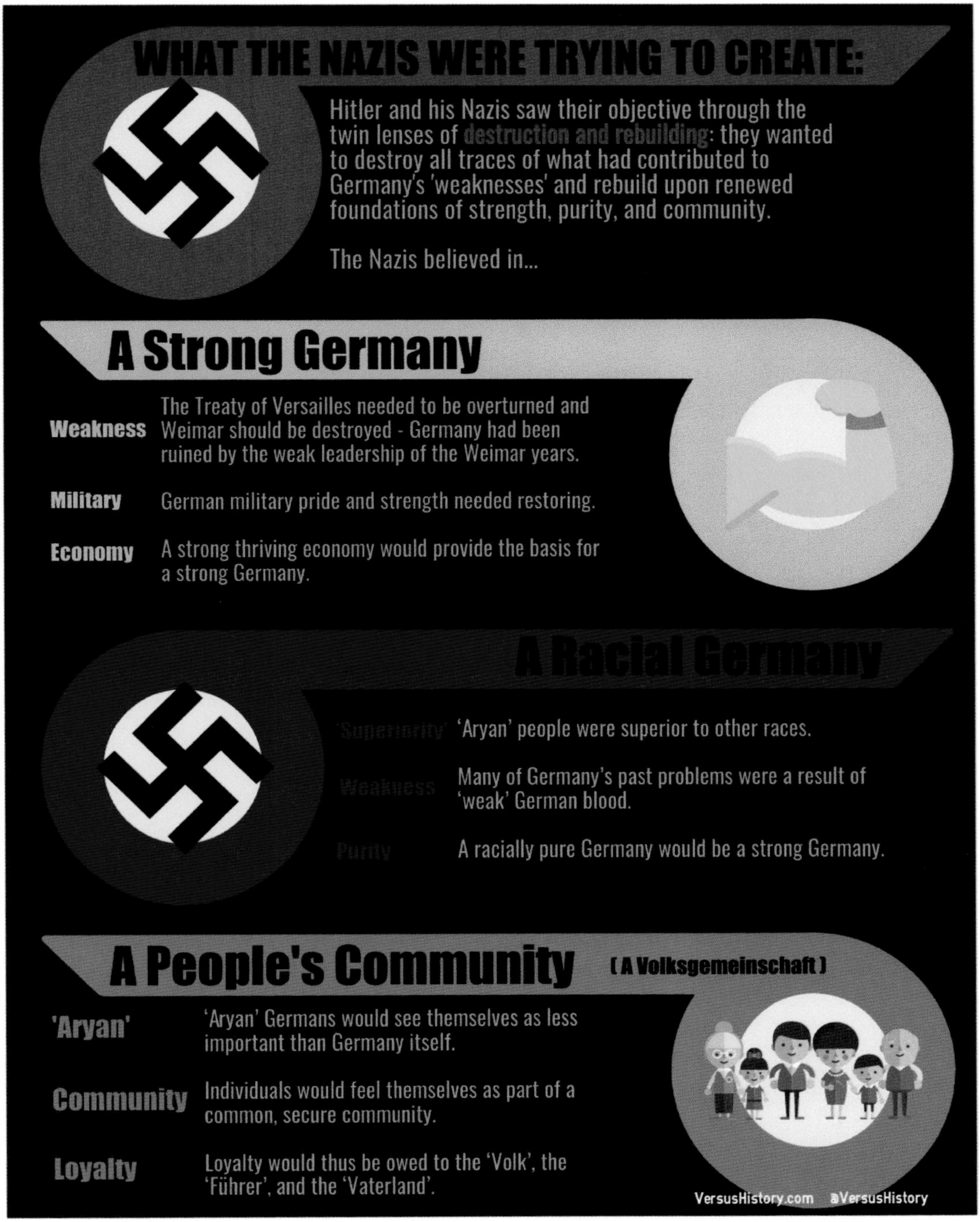
WHAT THE NAZIS WERE TRYING TO CREATE:
Hitler and his Nazis saw their objective through the twin lenses of destruction and rebuilding: they wanted to destroy all traces of what had contributed to Germany's 'weaknesses' and rebuild upon renewed foundations of strength, purity, and community.
The Nazis believed in...
A Strong Germany
Weakness
The Treaty of Versailles needed to be overturned and Weimar should be destroyed - Germany had been ruined by the weak leadership of the Weimar years.
Military
German military pride and strength needed restoring.
Economy
A strong thriving economy would provide the basis for a strong Germany.
A Racial Germany
'Superiority'
'Aryan' people were superior to other races.
Weakness
Many of Germany's past problems were a result of 'weak' German blood.
Purity
A racially pure Germany would be a strong Germany.
A People's Community
(A Volksgemeinschaft)
'Aryan'
'Aryan' Germans would see themselves as less important than Germany itself.
Community
Individuals would feel themselves as part of a common, secure community.
Loyalty
Loyalty would thus be owed to the 'Volk', the 'Führer', and the 'Vaterland'.
VersusHistory.com @VersusHistory

A discriminatory community

Overview

Nazi ideals did not allow for 'lukewarm' support. Either you were 'in', which meant you were expected to proactively support the creation of a new Germany, or else you were 'out' and in need of removal from society. To the Nazis only those who conformed would be allowed to take part in the creation of a glorious Volksgemeinschaft or 'people's community' which would renew and strengthen Germany. Within this new community, the individual's meaning and purpose was to be found in service of the nation rather than the self.

Significance

Achieving the Volksgemeinschaft was at the heart of the Nazi state. The main theme in endless propaganda, Germans were called upon to work together in order to strengthen the Fatherland, being prepared to sacrifice their wants and desires for the 'greater good'. This might involve women 'patriotically' working in a factory as part of the Duty Year program supporting rearmament, or young boys undergoing military training to strengthen the Wehrmacht in the future. Yet achieving the Volksgemeinschaft was to have its most significant and harrowing effects on those who, in Nazi eyes, threatened its creation. The creeping horrors experienced by homosexuals, gypsies and Jews, as well as people with disabilities, were rooted in this perception. Portrayed as diluting the 'purity of German blood' or lowering moral standards, it was believed that their removal was not only desirable, but necessary, if Germany was to gain strength, glory and honour.

Historiography

"Without a doubt, the production of the Volksgemeinschaft was a process of social inclusion that was supported by promises of equality, economic prosperity and symbolic recognition. Yet at the same time, Volksgemeinschaft meant dictatorial coercion, concentration camps and secret state police."

Michael Vildt
Hitler's Volksgemeinschaft and the Dynamics of Racial Exclusion (tr. B Heise)

Where to find out more

Visions of Community in Nazi Germany: Social Engineering and Private Lives
Martina Steber & Bernhard Gotto (eds.)

Nazism and German Society 1933-45
David F. Crew (ed.)

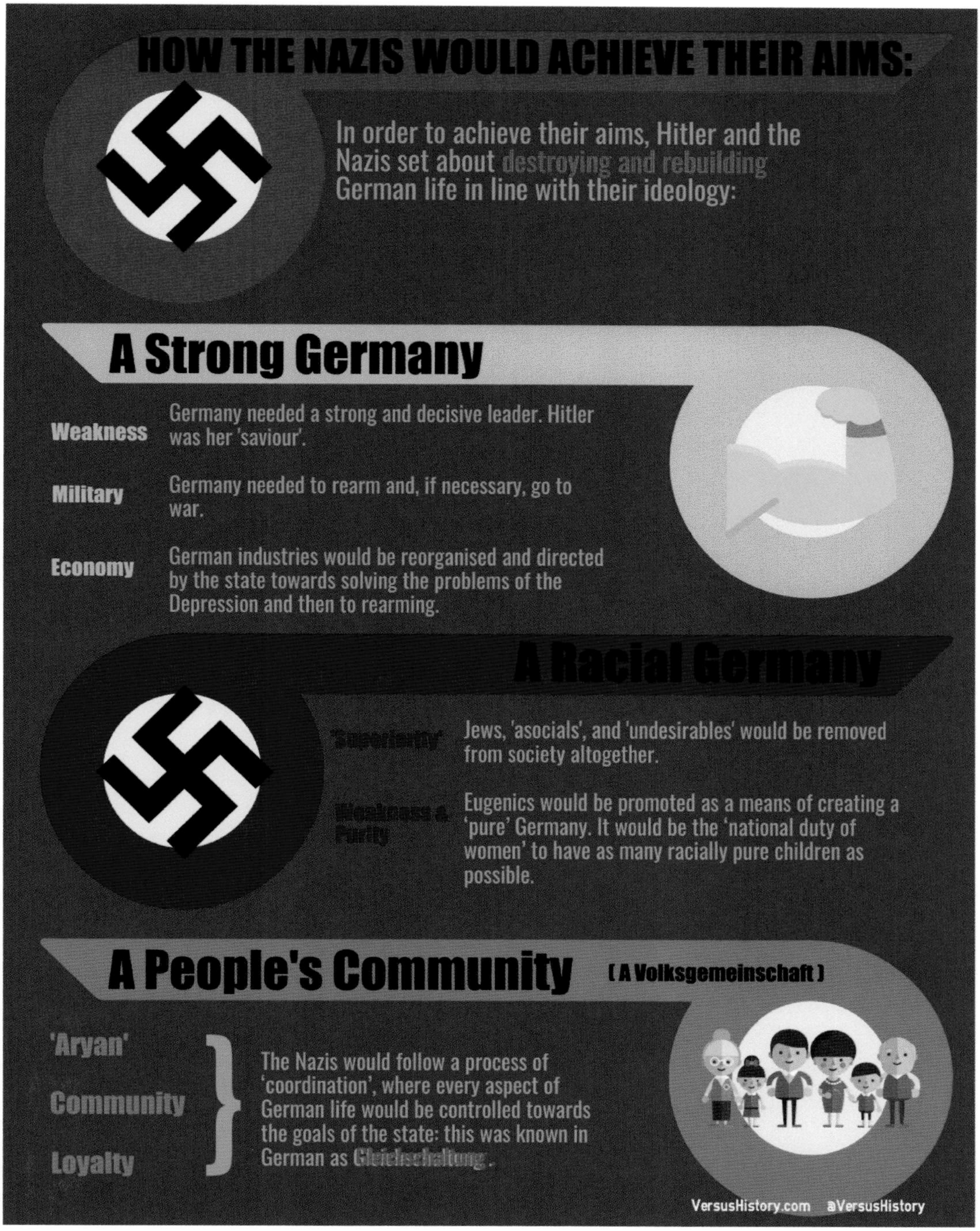
HOW THE NAZIS WOULD ACHIEVE THEIR AIMS:
In order to achieve their aims, Hitler and the Nazis set about destroying and rebuilding German life in line with their ideology:
A Strong Germany
Weakness
Germany needed a strong and decisive leader. Hitler was her 'saviour'.
Military
Germany needed to rearm and, if necessary, go to war.
Economy
German industries would be reorganised and directed by the state towards solving the problems of the Depression and then to rearming.
A Racial Germany
'Superiority'
Jews, 'asocials', and 'undesirables' would be removed from society altogether.
Weakness & Purity
Eugenics would be promoted as a means of creating a 'pure' Germany. It would be the 'national duty of women' to have as many racially pure children as possible.
A People's Community
[A Volksgemeinschaft]
'Aryan'
Community
Loyalty
The Nazis would follow a process of 'coordination', where every aspect of German life would be controlled towards the goals of the state: this was known in German as Gleichschaltung.
VersusHistory.com
@VersusHistory

Control by any other name

Overview

Control is the ultimate aim of the ruling class in any totalitarian regime. Totalitarianism requires that the ideology of those in power be so enmeshed within the very fabric of the institutional and individual spheres of existence, that it becomes impossible for human interactions *not* to be governed by it. National Socialism was the ideology of Germany from 1933-1945; Gleichschaltung was the method by which it was to be imposed. On everybody. Gleichschaltung was the word used to describe a unique blending of methods designed to control, coordinate, synchronise, and *Nazify* the population of Germany. From employment to leisure, from politics to business, from sex to religion, the Nazis sought coordination. Implicit in the meaning of Gleichschaltung was the understanding that any element of German society that could *not* be coordinated would be destroyed.

Significance

Conformity in Nazi Germany was not universal. Though it was profoundly impacting on the people of Germany, Gleichschaltung was not wholly successful and, in a number of instances, it was haphazard. Many areas of life remained firmly outside of the control of the National Socialists, for example the Catholic religion. Having said this, *all* those living in Germany experienced Gleichschaltung in one form or another. Incessant propaganda demonised 'enemies' while simultaneously emphasising, what Claudia Koonz termed, a "we-consciousness" that called for national unity, sacrifice, and loyalty to the Führer. The sum of these concerted attempts at coordination was that the Nazis came close, in some quarters, to the total destruction of individual identity within Germany. Gleichschaltung could be seen in the very language of the Third Reich: if a day was blessed with sunshine it was termed a day of "Hitler weather" (Viktor Klemperer).

Historiography

"...the speed and aggressive assertiveness of the National Socialist project of Gleichschaltung generated novel (and higher) standards of total coordination that outshone the Italian model."

Aristotle Kallis

Nazi Propaganda and 'Coordination': The Haphazard Path to Totalitarianism

Where to find out more

The Language of the Third Reich
Viktor Klemperer

The Nazi Conscience
Claudia Koonz

GLEICHSCHALTUNG
VersusHistory.com @VersusHistory
The Economy
To solve the problems of the Great Depression as well as achieve the goal of rearmament. Hjalmar Schacht tried to accomplish the former; Hermann Göring, the latter.
Young People & Education
To create an unquestioning loyalty through educational indoctrination and organisations such as the Hitler Youth.
Race
To create a racially pure Germany through exclusion, eugenics, murder and genocide.
'Gleichschaltung'
COORDINATION
Nazi totalitarianism required the 'coordination' of every aspect of German life.
Work & Leisure
To create a productive & indoctrinated population. The state would control all aspects of work and many aspects of leisure time.
Women & Family
To create (literally) future generations of loyal Nazis. Enshrined in the '3 K's': Kinder, Küche, Kirche (children, kitchen, church).
Religion
To create an alternative system of devotion - to the Nazis - using tools such as Mein Kampf, 'positive Christianity', propaganda, concentration camps and executions.
TOTALITARIANISM: A system of government that requires complete subservience to a ruler or ruling group. The ruler/group has TOTAL control over the population.
METHOD: Coordination - or gleichschaltung - of every aspect of German life.

Mind control

Overview

Propaganda – information that is designed and transmitted with the intention of influencing the opinions of people – was not a new thing to the governments of the world in the 1920's and 1930's. Its use is well documented throughout history. The Nazis relied heavily upon propaganda for such things as acquiring power, staying in power, gaining support for their policies, creating the cult of the leader, and disseminating their racist beliefs. From the swastika to the Nuremberg rallies, from *Der Stürmer* to cheap radios, from *Mein Kampf* to the *Blood Flag*, the National Socialists, under the guidance of Josef Goebbels, became masters of influence.

Significance

It is no overstatement to suggest that the Nazi use of propaganda was not merely crucial in their securing of power but that it was also an absolute necessity in their consolidation and maintenance of it. National Socialist propaganda – particularly once in power – accomplished four broad tasks: 1) It identified and demonised its enemies; 2) It indoctrinated German men, women and children in keeping with the ideology of National Socialism; 3) It promoted the need for Hitler's policies; 4) It tried to maintain morale during the war. Despite losing some of its potency during the war, Nazi propaganda was precedent-setting in the way that states control their populations. Their use of symbols, imagery and new technology (radios and such) became the benchmark by which totalitarian states would evaluate their own success in controlling their people.

Historiography

"Of all the new weapons and tactics employed by Nazi Germany prior and during World War II, propaganda was one of the most important..."

Michael J. Stout
The Effectiveness of Nazi Propaganda During World War Two.

Where to find out more

Blowing up the Nazis (chapters 2, 4 & 6)
Elliott L. Watson

Triumph of the Will (film)
Leni Riefenstahl

Nazi Propaganda and the Volksgemeinschaft
David Welch

NAZI PROPAGANDA BY THE NUMBERS

The man behind Nazi Propaganda was **Joseph Goebbels**.

In 1933 he was made **Reich Minister for Public Enlightenment and Propaganda**.

1,300

The number of films released by the Nazis between 1933-45.

After June 1935, the Propaganda Minister could block any film from being released "based on the public well-being".

2,500

The number of writers who left Germany by 1939 as a result of Nazi censorship. Guidelines of 'Un-German' themes for books were issued in May 1933.

35 marks

The cheapest radio available in Nazi Germany - the basic version of the VE301 - cost the equivalent of a week's wage. This allowed huge numbers to be sold. 70% of homes had one by 1939.

After March 1933 all broadcasts were centrally controlled.

42,000

The number of artists accepted into the Reich Chamber of Visual Arts. Without membership, artists were forbidden from teaching or selling their works.

500,000

The approximate number of copies of Der Stürmer published in 1937.

Der Stürmer was a weekly tabloid-style Nazi newspaper that was profoundly anti-Semitic.

6

The number of Nazi Party rallies held in Nuremberg between 1933-38.

The 1938 rally lasted a week and was attended by over 1 million people.

www.VersusHistory.com @VersusHistory

A state of control

Overview

Once Hitler established his dictatorship in the years 1933-1934, he needed to ensure that his power could not be threatened and that loyalty to the new Führer would be absolute. In order to accomplish this a state apparatus was constructed that tolerated no opposition from the German population and brutally enforced Hitler's rule. The main arms of this apparatus were the SS (incorporating the intelligence-gathering wing, the SD), the Gestapo, a network of concentration camps (and later, death camps), and the legal/justice systems. Through these mechanisms, freedoms were erased in the name of the 'common good', 'crimes' needed no due process, guilt was adjudged to be anything interpreted as being in contradiction of National Socialism, and punishments were arbitrary and swift.

Significance

It cannot be overstated just how fundamental to Hitler's dictatorship the police state was. As counter factual as it may be, without the complex systems of control exemplified by the SS, the SD, and the Gestapo, it is possible to imagine a German history in which Hitler's rule was even shorter than it turned out to be. In almost every aspect of German life there was a coordinated brutality; within the legal as well as the 'extra-judicial' realms so crucial to the successful functioning of a 'just' society, there was embedded ideology and violence. That is not to say that the police state wielded its violence bluntly and indiscriminately – it was mostly targeted and discriminate. However, fear *was* a constant and the German people understood the consequences of opposition. Accompanied by smothering propaganda, the police state became the very foundation of Nazi control.

Historiography

"...long before the destruction of German cities by Allied bombs, the German nation herself... had destroyed... the respect for the law, the clean hands of the judiciary..."

Maximilian Koessler
The Debasement of Germany's Legal System

Where to find out more

The Gestapo
Frank McDonough

Backing Hitler: Consent and Coercion in Nazi Germany
Robert Gellately

Destroyed opposition & provided security
Fought as combat units during the war
Carried out racial policies
Ran the concentration & extermination camps
Organised the 'Final Solution'
THE SS (SCHUTZSTAFFEL)
VersusHistory.com @VersusHistory
Monitored, prosecuted, and executed opponents
Created fear and paranoia
Helped organise the Holocaust
Gathered intelligence on opponents
Was not hindered by legal or judicial oversight
Persuaded people to inform on others
THE GESTAPO (SECRET POLICE)
THE NAZI POLICE STATE
Sondergericht (special courts) operated outside of the ordinary judicial system
12,000 executed by 'special courts'
No appeals courts
Nazi laws removed Jews from civic life
Used to justify all NSDAP actions
Volksgerichtshof (People's Court) dealt with 'treason'
Used to remove opposition 'legally'
LAW & COURTS
Used to imprison & torture opponents of the regime
Spread across conquered territory during the war
Used to carry out the Holocaust
Some used as labour camps
Housed so-called 'asocials' & 'deviants'
Dachau was the first concentration camp
CAMPS

Helping Hitler

Overview

From Walter Funk to Heinrich Himmler, Adolf Hitler relied upon a great number of men (and the occasional woman) to carry out his directions – both those he explicitly stated and those he implied. Some of these men, such as Albert Speer - Hitler's Chief Architect and Minister for Armaments – operated more on the fringes of the extremism carried out by the Nazis, however, many others were central to the horrors ultimately perpetrated in the name of National Socialism. Some, like Himmler and Goebbels, were deeply fanatical, whereas others were more, for want of a better word, pragmatic. *All* were involved in creating and sustaining the Third Reich, and without them it would never have functioned in the manner that it did.

Significance

The Nuremberg Trials that took place after World War Two were a mechanism by which those involved in the barbarism of the Third Reich would be held to account. They also help us understand just how central these individuals were to Hitler's vision. Hitler was a poor administrator and required his subordinates to interpret, plan, and execute his wishes – what Kershaw termed, *working towards the Führer*. Consequently, many Nazi policies – both those pedestrian as well as hideous in nature – bear the clear signature of those individuals who carried them out. The architecture of the Third Reich was the unmistakable progeny of Albert Speer; the indelible fingerprints of the monstrous Heinrich Himmler and Reinhard Heydrich can be found all over the *Final Solution*.

Historiography

"...Hitler is absolutely crucial...But the actual practical steps are taken by his leading figures..."

Ian Kershaw
Interview by Laurence Rees: Hitler and the Holocaust

Where to find out more

Hitler's Circle of Evil
Drama/Documentary

In the Garden of Beasts
Erik Larson

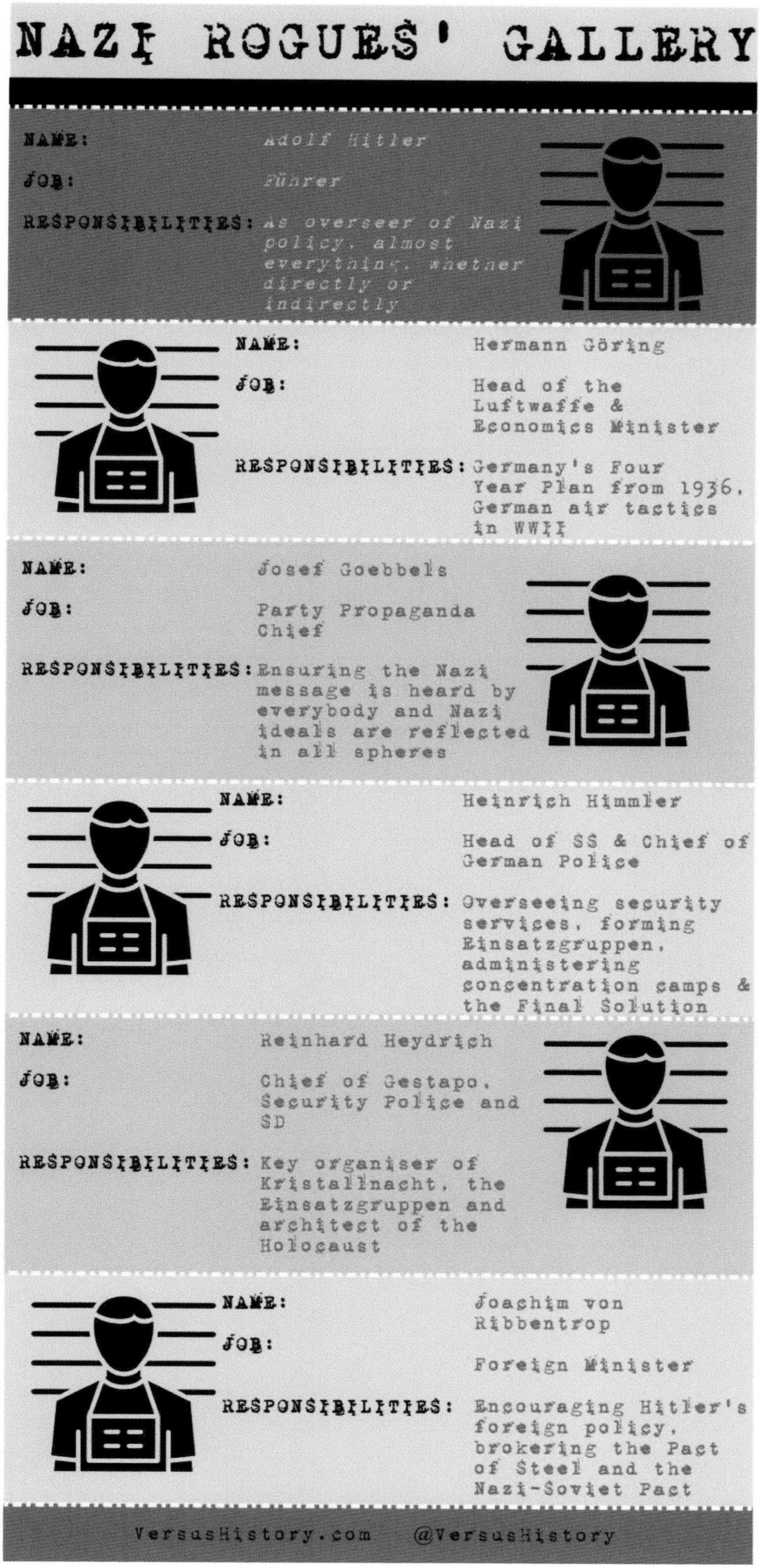
NAZI ROGUES' GALLERY
NAME: Adolf Hitler
JOB: Führer
RESPONSIBILITIES: As overseer of Nazi policy, almost everything, whether directly or indirectly
NAME: Hermann Göring
JOB: Head of the Luftwaffe & Economics Minister
RESPONSIBILITIES: Germany's Four Year Plan from 1936, German air tactics in WWII
NAME: Josef Goebbels
JOB: Party Propaganda Chief
RESPONSIBILITIES: Ensuring the Nazi message is heard by everybody and Nazi ideals are reflected in all spheres
NAME: Heinrich Himmler
JOB: Head of SS & Chief of German Police
RESPONSIBILITIES: Overseeing security services, forming Einsatzgruppen, administering concentration camps & the Final Solution
NAME: Reinhard Heydrich
JOB: Chief of Gestapo, Security Police and SD
RESPONSIBILITIES: Key organiser of Kristallnacht, the Einsatzgruppen and architect of the Holocaust
NAME: Joachim von Ribbentrop
JOB: Foreign Minister
RESPONSIBILITIES: Encouraging Hitler's foreign policy, brokering the Pact of Steel and the Nazi-Soviet Pact
VersusHistory.com @VersusHistory

Giving birth to the future

Overview

Hitler envisaged a Germany of two clearly defined sexual spheres: one in which men dominated and fought; one in which women gave birth and nurtured the family. To the Führer, this was the 'natural order'. Nazi ideology, policy, propaganda, and Hitler himself encouraged women to focus only on a 'traditional' version of femininity and womanhood. This version involved staying home, having 'racially pure' children, using leftovers of every kind in order to create a self-sufficient household, and looking after her husband. The *Mother's Cross of Honour* promoted childbearing, laws passed in 1936 began removing women from a variety of employments, while the *Bund Deutscher Mädel* and the *Frauenschaft* provided for the ideological 'grounding' of young women.

Significance

While there is no homogenous experience of women under the Nazis, and more recent historiography explores the agency of German women, it is without question that they were expected to serve a very specific remit for the National Socialists: that of broodmare for the state. The future of Hitler's Germany was foundationally dependent upon the ability and desire of 'racially pure' German women to produce the desired *Aryan* children, for they were the future of a Reich that would last one thousand years. Boys would be the loyal soldiers; girls the loyal progenitors of a 'superior' race. However, much of this changed once the demands of the war became clear and many women were forced into industry.

Historiography

"...we know today that the Frauenbewegung (women's movement) thought the place of a woman in society was at the heart of a community that excluded Jews and performed a civilizing mission in occupied Eastern Europe to preserve the race."

Marie-Bénédicte Incent
History of German Society in the 20th Century

Where to find out more

Hitler's Furies: Women of the Third Reich Holocaust Living History
Wendy Lower

Women in Nazi Germany
Jill Stephenson

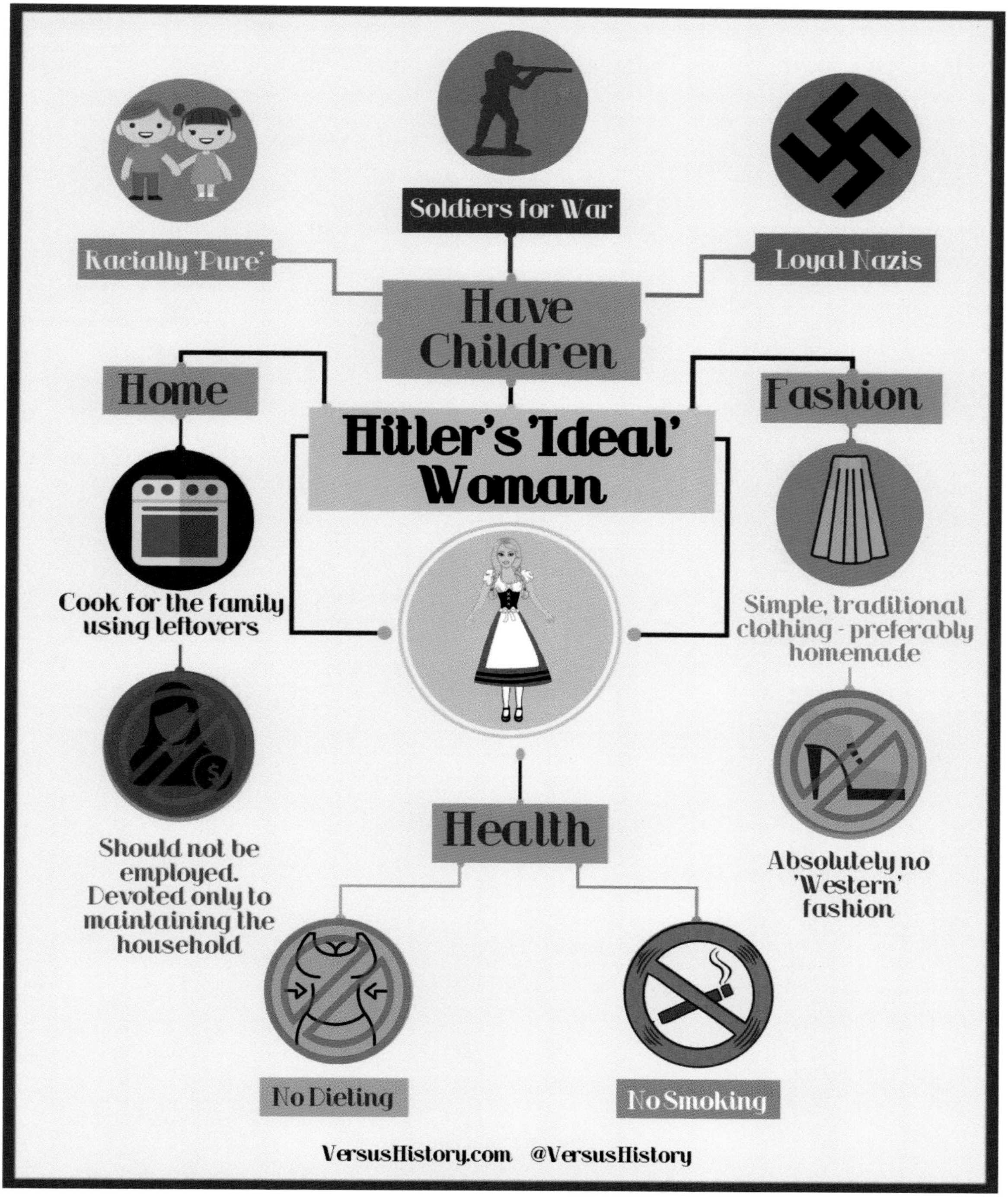
Soldiers for War
Racially 'Pure'
Loyal Nazis
Have Children
Home
Fashion
Hitler's 'Ideal' Woman
Cook for the family using leftovers
Simple, traditional clothing - preferably homemade
Should not be employed. Devoted only to maintaining the household
Health
Absolutely no 'Western' fashion
No Dieting
No Smoking
VersusHistory.com @VersusHistory

Lessons in loyalty

Overview

Hitler optimistically believed his Reich would last a thousand years. The foundation of this Third Reich, as Hitler saw it, would be the 'racially pure' young people of Germany. As a means of resetting Germany's historical clock and beginning anew, Hitler sought to indoctrinate the youth as early as possible. In doing so, Hitler hoped to create a new order of German people, unswerving in their loyalty and total in their devotion – willing to carry out the most repellent of orders because they were utterly convinced of the rectitude of the Führer's plans. Consequently, German education was restructured so that boys were prepared for combat, struggle and sacrifice, whereas girls were to be mothers and wives.

Significance

According to Edward J. Kenner, "The submission of individuals to the will of… a strong *Führer* is not new". Germans had spent much of the previous thousand years submitting to strong leaders – in fact, to many, it was a source of great pride. As a result, that they accepted an educational system promoting nationalism and sacrifice should not be cause for surprise. The failures of Weimar and the onset of the Great Depression should reduce surprise even further still; in the eyes of many Germans, democracy had brought rack and ruin. A return to the authoritarianism of the past was welcomed – by adults and children alike. What *was* different about the Nazi control of education, was what they were able to achieve with it: it was the young men of the SS that carried out the most heinous of Hitler's orders.

Historiography

"(Schools)…represented… the Nazi Weltanschauung by fostering the leadership principle, promoting competitiveness, and emphasizing life as a struggle and survival of the fittest."

Lisa Pine
Education in Nazi Germany

Where to find out more

School for Barbarians: Education Under the Nazis
Erika Mann

Higher Education in Nazi Germany
Professor A. Wolf

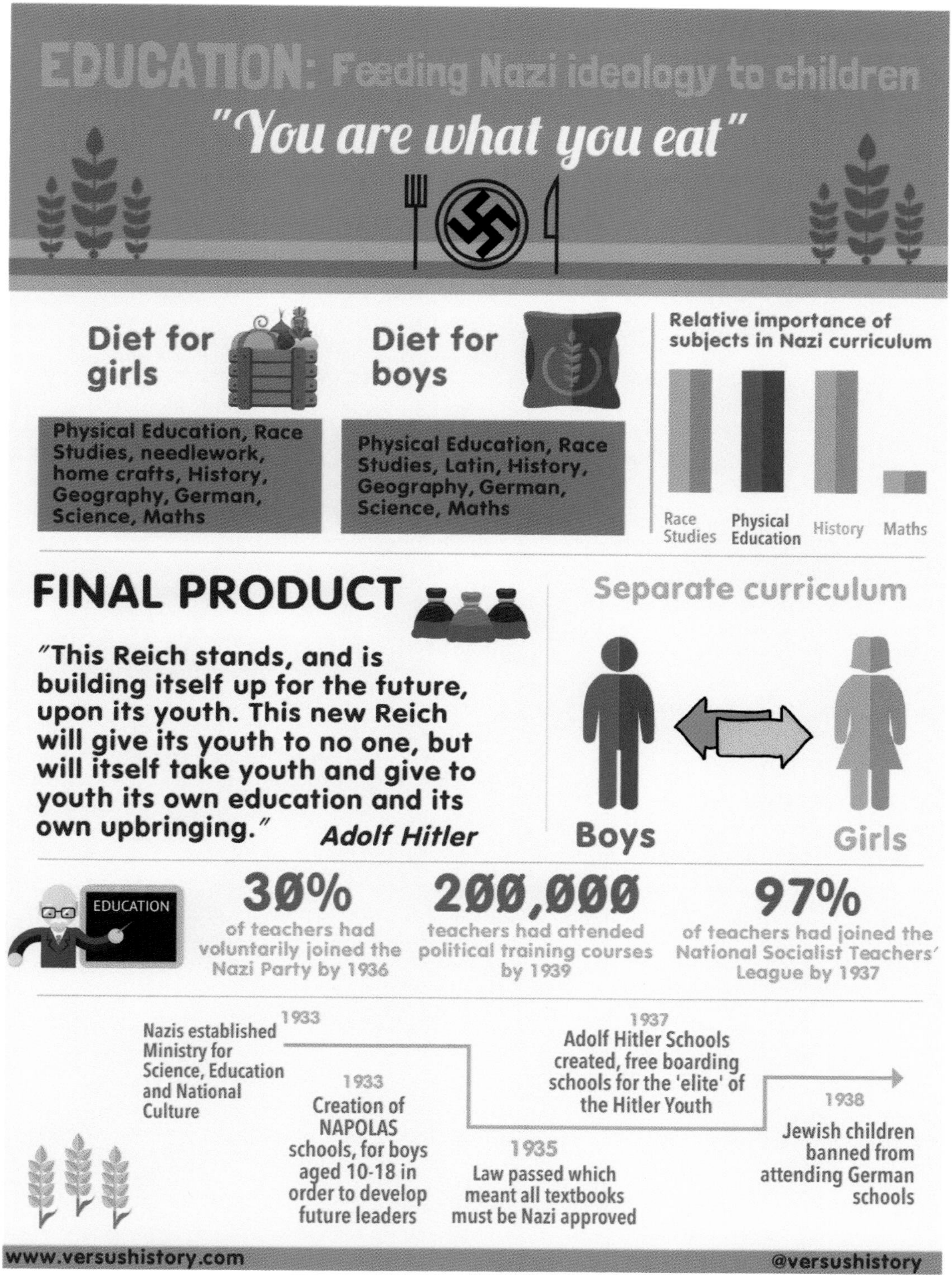
EDUCATION: Feeding Nazi ideology to children
"You are what you eat"
Diet for girls
Physical Education, Race Studies, needlework, home crafts, History, Geography, German, Science, Maths
Diet for boys
Physical Education, Race Studies, Latin, History, Geography, German, Science, Maths
Relative importance of subjects in Nazi curriculum
Race Studies
Physical Education
History
Maths
FINAL PRODUCT
"This Reich stands, and is building itself up for the future, upon its youth. This new Reich will give its youth to no one, but will itself take youth and give to youth its own education and its own upbringing." Adolf Hitler
Separate curriculum
Boys
Girls
EDUCATION
30% of teachers had voluntarily joined the Nazi Party by 1936
200,000 teachers had attended political training courses by 1939
97% of teachers had joined the National Socialist Teachers' League by 1937
1933 Nazis established Ministry for Science, Education and National Culture
1933 Creation of NAPOLAS schools, for boys aged 10-18 in order to develop future leaders
1935 Law passed which meant all textbooks must be Nazi approved
1937 Adolf Hitler Schools created, free boarding schools for the 'elite' of the Hitler Youth
1938 Jewish children banned from attending German schools
www.versushistory.com
@versushistory

A growing concern

Overview

It is a recurring truism in all societies that children are the future. Nazi Germany was no different, Hitler himself said in 1933 "I am beginning with the young. We older ones are used up….with them I can make a new world". Influencing and winning over the youth was a central plank in creating the Volksgemeinschaft and ensuring that the Nazis would succeed in their aims of establishing a 'Thousand Year Reich'. Whether at school or at leisure the young were exposed to Nazi ideas and either encouraged, coerced or compelled, depending on the situation, to reflect these.

Significance

In vying for the loyalty of the youth, the Nazi Party were not alone. Parents, schools and religious groups all had influence that needed to be mitigated or removed. Nazi youth organizations were at the heart of this drive. From the age of 10, youngsters were inducted into the Deutsches Jungvolk or the Jungmädelbund, before graduating to the Hitler Youth or League of German Maidens, both of which took members up until age 18. The organizations laid on activities and offered freedom from parents, but they also sought to create an identity emphasizing the youth's critical importance to the nation. The regime was not above employing underhand tactics; from 1936 for example, membership was made compulsory. The extremely small-scale nature of youth resistance groups such as the Swing Youth and the Edelweiss Pirates suggest a significant degree of Nazi success when compared to the millions within Nazi youth organisations. More harrowing still are the reports of the fanaticism demonstrated by Hitler Youth members as young as 12 in the forlorn defense of Berlin in 1945.

Historiography

"Whether they joined freely or by force of law, whether they believed fully in the Führer's cause or merely said they did because everyone else seemed to say so, whether they actively promoted Nazism or actively resisted it, they were all members of the Hitler Youth generation…"

Gerhard Rempel
Hitler's Children: The Hitler Youth and the SS

Where to find out more

Hitler Youth
M. Cater

German Voices: Memories of Life during Hitler's Third Reich
F.C. Turbach

7 WAYS TO GROW NAZI YOUTHS
SECURING THE FUTURE
KEEP THEM BUSY
EXPOSE THEM TO YOUR IDEAS CONSTANTLY
SEND THEM TO THE GREAT OUTDOORS
GIVE THEM UNIFORMS AND AN IDENTITY
10
PRIORITISE COMRADESHIP
MAKE MEMBERSHIP COMPULSORY
TELL THEM THEY ARE THE FUTURE
VersusHistory.com @VersusHistory

By the numbers

Overview

When Hitler became chancellor in 1933, the German economy was mired in a crisis of international debt, catastrophic unemployment of over 30%, and rising inflation. Hitler and the National Socialists had promised an 'economic miracle' if they were given power and so they quickly set about the task of returning Germany's economy to a position of stability. They did this through a number of methods, most significantly they invested in massive public works schemes and rearmament. Both of these methods were supported by the control of workers through such organisations as the RAD and DAF, as well as by manipulating the unemployment figures – women, Jews, and many young men were excluded from the unemployment register. As President of the Reichsbank and then Minister of Economics, Hjalmar Schacht's priority was combatting the effects of the Great Depression. This priority would later be replaced by a focus on rearmament, administered by Herman Göring with his Four Year Plan.

Significance

Issues relating to the Nazi economy continue to fuel debate amongst historians. From the motivations driving economic policy to evaluations of its achievements, lines have been drawn and arguments made. By and large it is agreed that the National Socialists did achieve success in reducing unemployment through rearmament and public works. It is also agreed that they did so by 'reclassifying' who could be termed unemployed. The war economy generated significant employment – expenditure on the military rose from 1% to 10% of Germany's national income in the first two years of Hitler's rule, and to almost 75% in 1945 – but as the tide of war turned against Germany, the engine driving the economy ground to a halt. When this happened, no amount of propaganda could persuade the German people of an 'economic miracle'.

Historiography

"The Nazi government substituted conscious, over-all direction of the economy for the autonomy of the market mechanism and subordinated the economic system to a predetermined objective, the creation of a war machine."

Otto Nathan
Nazi War Finance and Banking

Where to find out more

The Structure of the Nazi Economy
Maxine Y. Sweezy

Mein Kampf Vol II, Chapter XII 'The Trade Union Question'
Adolf Hitler

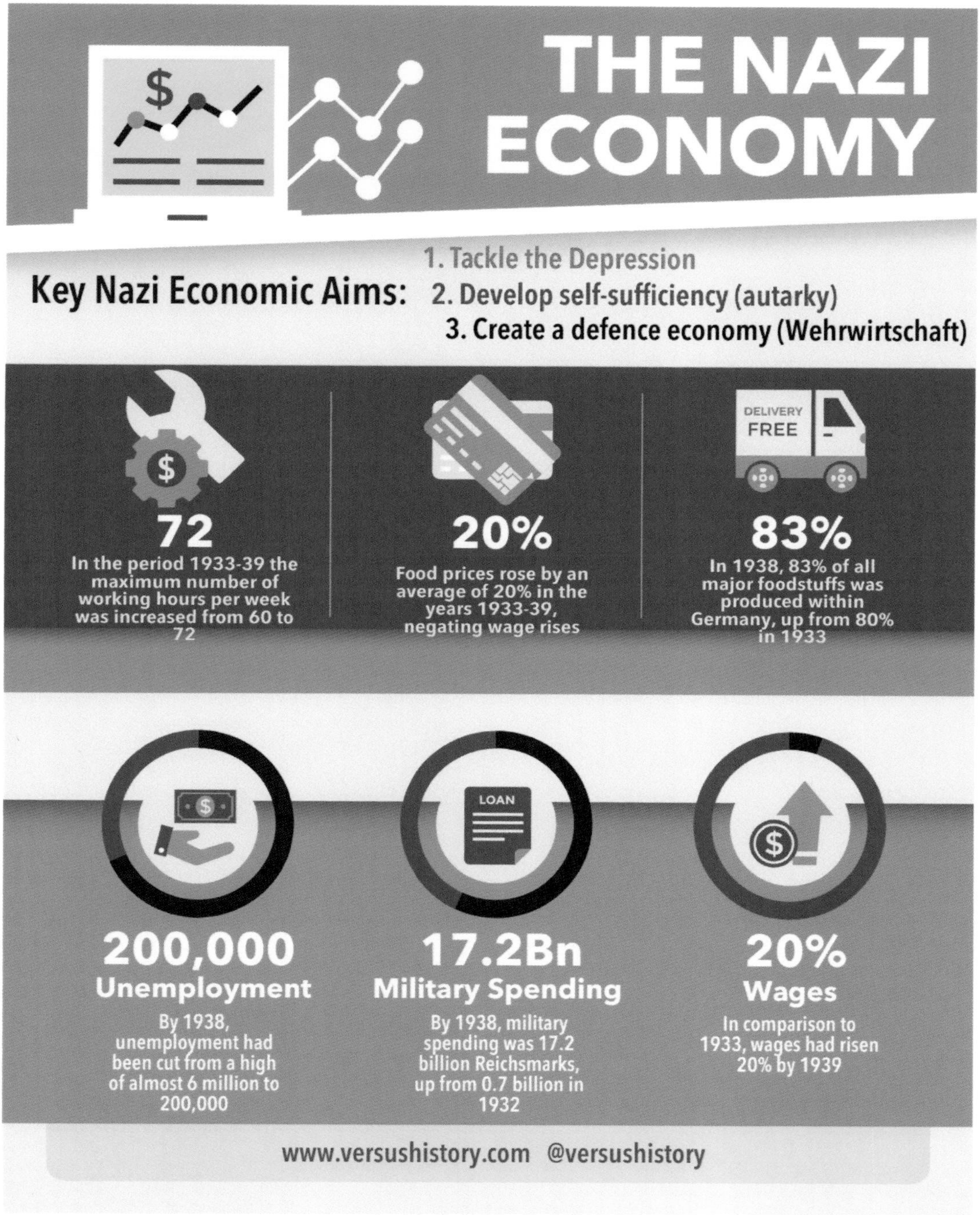
THE NAZI ECONOMY
Key Nazi Economic Aims:
1. Tackle the Depression
2. Develop self-sufficiency (autarky)
3. Create a defence economy (Wehrwirtschaft)
72
In the period 1933-39 the maximum number of working hours per week was increased from 60 to 72
20%
Food prices rose by an average of 20% in the years 1933-39, negating wage rises
DELIVERY FREE
83%
In 1938, 83% of all major foodstuffs was produced within Germany, up from 80% in 1933
200,000
Unemployment
By 1938, unemployment had been cut from a high of almost 6 million to 200,000
LOAN
17.2Bn
Military Spending
By 1938, military spending was 17.2 billion Reichsmarks, up from 0.7 billion in 1932
20%
Wages
In comparison to 1933, wages had risen 20% by 1939
www.versushistory.com @versushistory

Unemployment off the menu

Overview

Hitler came to power in the middle of the greatest global economic crisis in history. Germany, having endured a grueling post-war period, was hit particularly hard as the fragility of Stresemann's economic reforms were exposed by the Wall Street Crash and the Great Depression. Hitler and the National Socialists had promised to solve the core economic problems affecting the German population, the most urgent of which was arguably unemployment. In 1933, approximately 30% (6 million) of the workforce was unemployed, yet by the time Hitler invaded Poland in September 1939, that figure was practically zero.

Significance

The Nazi employment 'miracle' – of almost eradicating unemployment in the Reich within six years of coming to power – is significant for two main reasons: 1) The methods they used to achieve it; 2) It proved to many Germans that they could deliver results. When Hitler passed the *Unemployment Relief Act* in June 1933, promising that unemployment would be eliminated within four years, he was pledging to do what the Weimar governments had been unable to do: deliver on promises of a return to sustained economic stability. By making good on those promises, the NSDAP would prove their legitimacy as a governing party. More than this, their success would contain an implied demand for the loyalty of the German people. Through public works schemes and rearmament, unemployment quickly began to disappear. By the time Hitler was proclaiming success in ridding Germany entirely of unemployment, many Germans were relatively content to ignore some of the methods used to achieve it: expelling Jews and women from the workforce, mandatory work service in the RAD, and control of the workforce.

Historiography

"The new government fully realized that it could win and keep the confidence of the masses only if it succeeded in decreasing unemployment as rapidly as possible."

Friedrich Baerwald
How Germany Reduced Unemployment

Where to find out more

The Nazi Economic Recovery, 1932-38
R.J. Overy

The Wages of Destruction
Adam Tooze

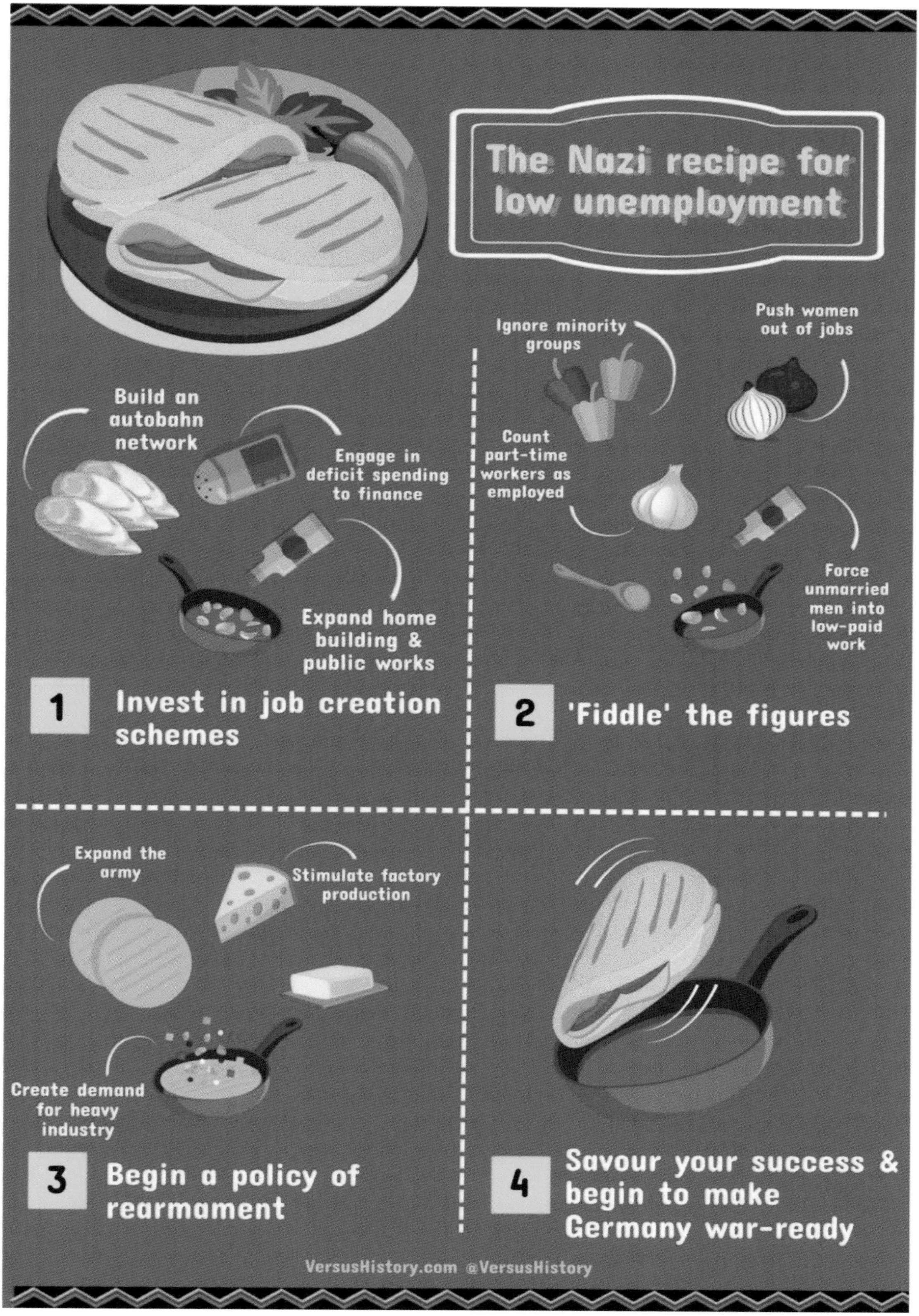
The Nazi recipe for low unemployment
Build an autobahn network
Engage in deficit spending to finance
Expand home building & public works
1 Invest in job creation schemes
Ignore minority groups
Push women out of jobs
Count part-time workers as employed
Force unmarried men into low-paid work
2 'Fiddle' the figures
Expand the army
Stimulate factory production
Create demand for heavy industry
3 Begin a policy of rearmament
4 Savour your success & begin to make Germany war-ready
VersusHistory.com @VersusHistory

Crossing the church

Overview

In any totalitarian regime, by definition, there can be no alternative authority other than the state to which people should owe obedience. The Protestant and Catholic religions had centuries of influence over the people of Germany, engendering a faithful devotion that would have to be challenged and then broken if the Nazis were to create a truly totalitarian Reich. When the National Socialists first came to power, their position was of relative weakness in the face of traditional German religious fidelity. Consequently, any assault on the German churches would have to wait until they felt in a secure enough position to mount one. Proof of this is the *Concordat* that was signed very early in Hitler's chancellorship. As they became more secure, attacks on religion escalated, with murderous effect. However, as Richard Evans wrote, even in 1939, 95% of Germans still identified as Catholic or Protestant.

Significance

Though the Nazi 25-Point Programme called for the toleration of Christian practices in Germany, all dominations were eventually targeted for 'coordination'. As the National Socialists became more secure in their power, criticism of, and then open hostility towards, the churches escalated quickly. Property was confiscated, youth organisations disbanded, and leaders were purged. An alternative 'Reich Church' and 'German Faith Movement' were created to draw the faithful away from the dominant religions. Although the history of the German churches under the Nazis is complex, perhaps it is significant to note two things: 1) Despite Nazi efforts, neither the Catholic nor Protestant faiths sustained any long-term institutional damage; 2) Much resistance to the Nazis came in the form of individual protests – such as those by Bishop von Galen and Pastor Niemöller; their efforts made all the more heroic by the fate that obviously awaited them.

Historiography

"...it seems that, for many Germans, adherence to the Christian faith proved compatible with at least passive acquiescence in, if not active support for, the Nazi dictatorship."

Mary Fulbrook
The Fontana History of Germany: 1918-1990

Where to find out more

The Catholic Church and the Holocaust, 1930-1965
Michael Phayer

The Nazi Persecution of the Churches, 1933-1845
John S. Conway

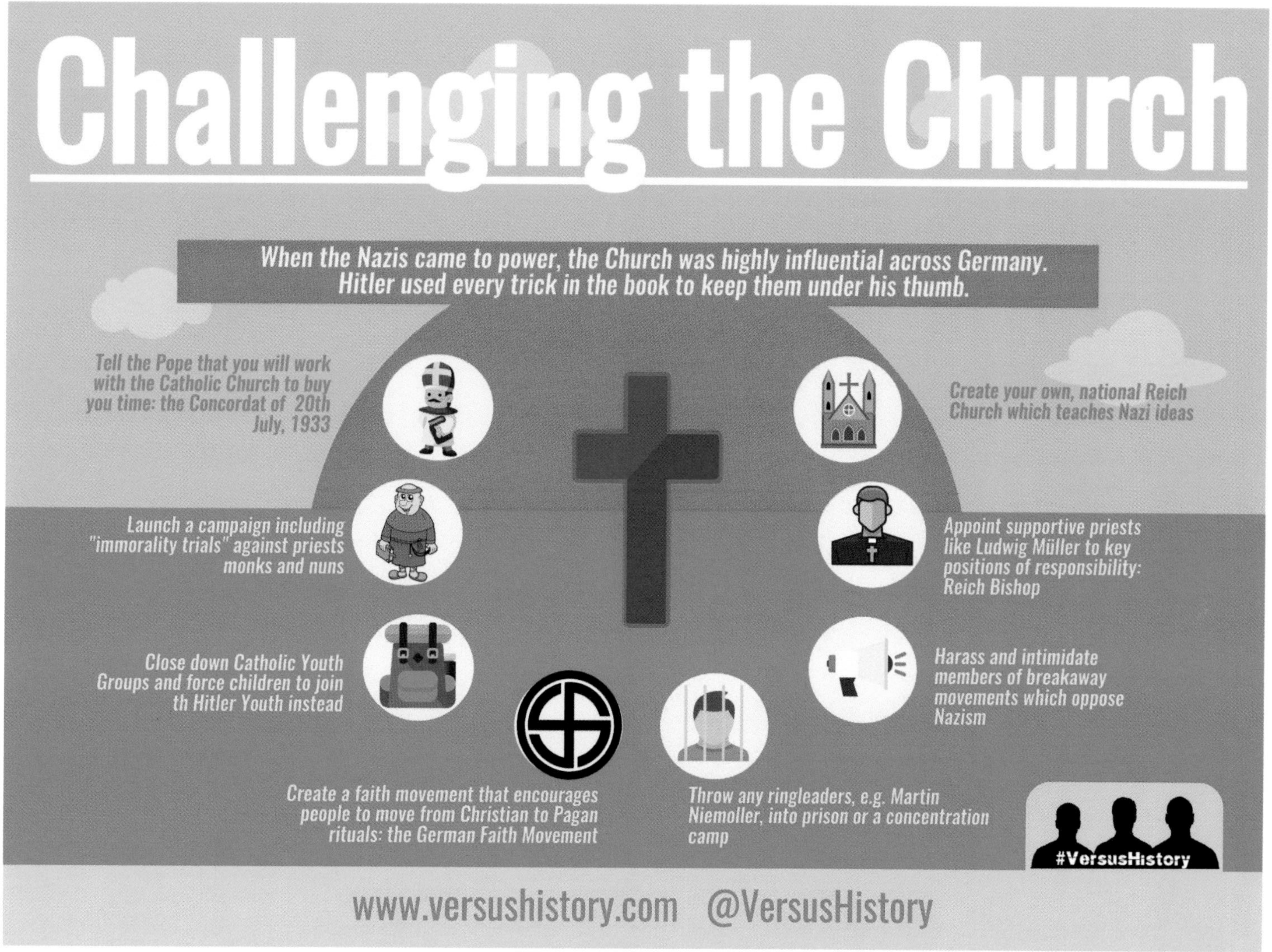
Challenging the Church
When the Nazis came to power, the Church was highly influential across Germany.
Hitler used every trick in the book to keep them under his thumb.
Tell the Pope that you will work with the Catholic Church to buy you time: the Concordat of 20th July, 1933
Create your own, national Reich Church which teaches Nazi ideas
Launch a campaign including "immorality trials" against priests monks and nuns
Appoint supportive priests like Ludwig Müller to key positions of responsibility: Reich Bishop
Close down Catholic Youth Groups and force children to join th Hitler Youth instead
Harass and intimidate members of breakaway movements which oppose Nazism
Create a faith movement that encourages people to move from Christian to Pagan rituals: the German Faith Movement
Throw any ringleaders, e.g. Martin Niemoller, into prison or a concentration camp
#VersusHistory
www.versushistory.com @VersusHistory

Minority report

Overview

Hitler's desire to create a *Volksgemeinschaft* – a People's Community of racially 'pure' Germans – necessitated (according to him) the removal of a great many individuals and groups that did not 'fit' into this community or were not 'productive' enough to contribute to it. Once in power, the National Socialists began almost immediately targeting minorities for either identification, persecution, separation or extermination. Sometimes they were targeted for all four. From the differently abled to homosexuals, from the 'work-shy' to Europe's Jews, vast swathes of humanity fell outside of Hitler's notion of a German Volksgemeinschaft.

Significance

Although the wholesale and vile extermination of Europe's Jews was very much a feature of the latter years of Nazi rule, persecution of minorities, including Germany's Jewish population, was an ever-present, constantly evolving feature of the National Socialist state. As early as July 1933, Hitler had begun to put his plans for the creation of a Volksgemeinschaft into action, with the *Law for the Prevention of Hereditarily Diseased Offspring*. This law set a precedent for the legal manipulation of Germany's 'racial hygiene' as German 'Health Courts' made existential decisions about those individuals brought before them. These 'courts' became increasingly more integrated into the state's machinery of minority persecution, highlighted by the T4 euthanasia programme which ultimately mutated into genocide. In totalitarian Nazi Germany, the escalating persecution of minorities was often 'accepted' by the general population because it was draped in the veil of the law. By the time millions were being killed, it was far too late to resist.

Historiography

"Genschel's work made clear that the expulsion and expropriation of the Jews was not sudden but gradual, a creeping process that went through several phases, radicalizing in spurts, until it culminated in November 1938 in the 'legal exclusion' of the Jews from economic life."

Frank Bajohr
Expropriation and Expulsion

Where to find out more

Asperger's Children: The Origins of Autism in Nazi Vienna
Edith Sheffer

The Nazi Persecution of the Gypsies
Guenter Lewy

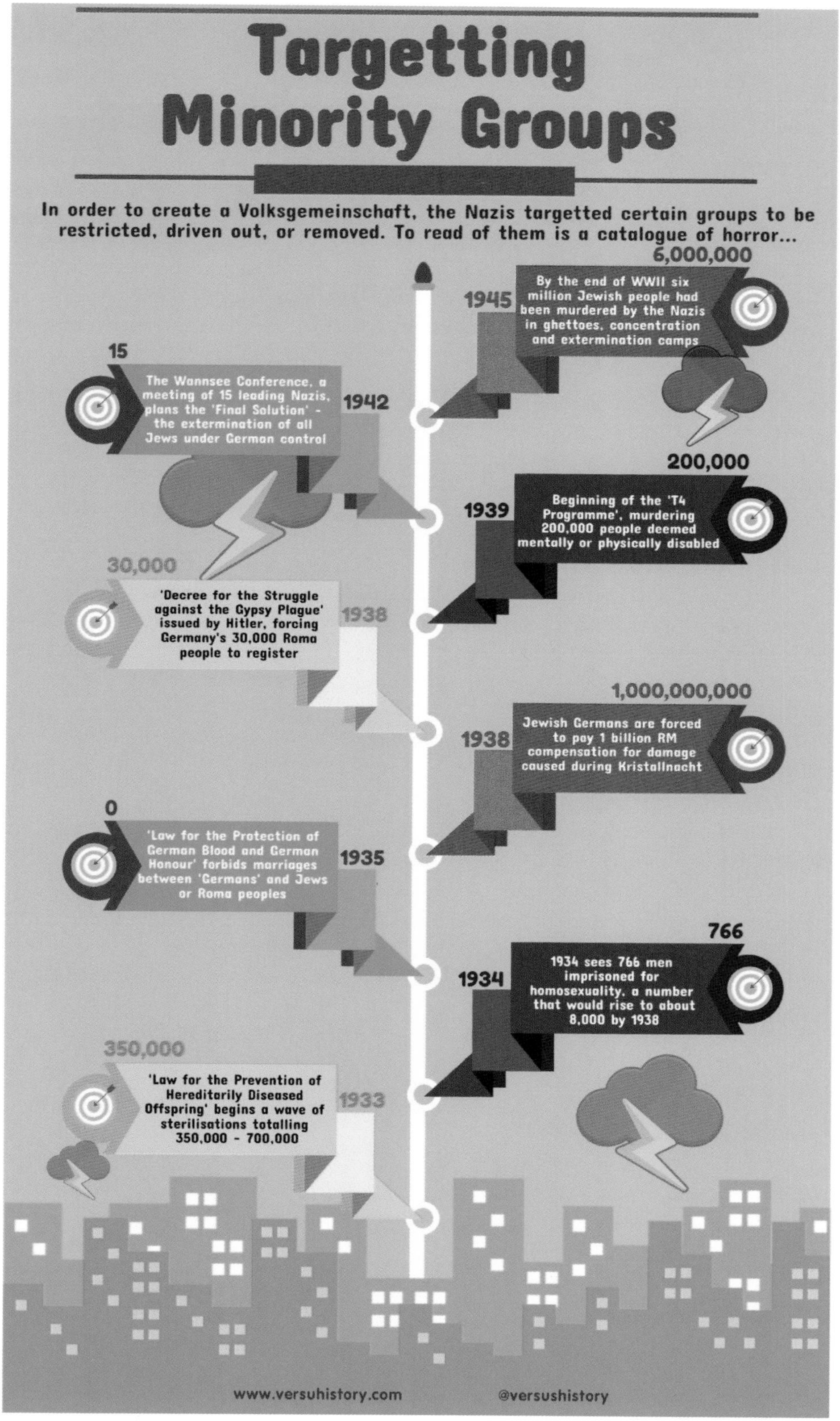
Targetting Minority Groups
In order to create a Volksgemeinschaft, the Nazis targetted certain groups to be restricted, driven out, or removed. To read of them is a catalogue of horror...
6,000,000
1945
By the end of WWII six million Jewish people had been murdered by the Nazis in ghettoes, concentration and extermination camps
15
1942
The Wannsee Conference, a meeting of 15 leading Nazis, plans the 'Final Solution' - the extermination of all Jews under German control
200,000
1939
Beginning of the 'T4 Programme', murdering 200,000 people deemed mentally or physically disabled
30,000
1938
'Decree for the Struggle against the Gypsy Plague' issued by Hitler, forcing Germany's 30,000 Roma people to register
1,000,000,000
1938
Jewish Germans are forced to pay 1 billion RM compensation for damage caused during Kristallnacht
0
1935
'Law for the Protection of German Blood and German Honour' forbids marriages between 'Germans' and Jews or Roma peoples
766
1934
1934 sees 766 men imprisoned for homosexuality, a number that would rise to about 8,000 by 1938
350,000
1933
'Law for the Prevention of Hereditarily Diseased Offspring' begins a wave of sterilisations totalling 350,000 - 700,000
www.versuhistory.com
@versushistory

Reducing resistance

Overview

In any totalitarian regime, absolute obedience is not just expected, it is mandatory, often on pain of death. Any evaluation into the success of Nazi totalitarianism must necessarily consider the extent to which people refused to cooperate or outright stood in opposition to National Socialist control. Of course, this is much easier said than done because most opposition was secretive, personal and small-scale; it was also, by and large, lacking in overall direction and cohesion: it was not united. Nonetheless, opposition *did* exist in many forms, from grumbling over dinner at home, to attempts to murder Hitler, and much in between the two.

Significance

It is a fact of life in Nazi Germany that during the years 1933-38, opposition was a rare thing. Many Germans were content to accept the NSDAP as long as they ameliorated the problems associated with the Great Depression. Further, a significant number agreed with elements of National Socialism. Looking back on Hitler's rule it is easy to see how the seeds of murder, genocide, and war were sown in clear actions taken by the regime, however, the horrors of the Nazis were, in the main, creeping and gradual. Few at the time could have pointed to any individual action by Hitler or his acolytes and stood in opposition to what it 'might' have led to. Nonetheless, opposition *did* occur – particularly when the war clouds gathered, the extermination of Europe's Jews began and, later, when the war became a lost cause. While much of it failed to shift the direction of National Socialism, *all* of it was courageous.

Historiography

"More important was the public policies of Nazi racism, which while being decried by churches and some members of society, more often than not "were accepted and even approved, provided that they were applied within a framework that was outwardly legal"."

Kevin Korst quoting Detlev J. K. Peukert
Nazism and the German People: A Historiography

Where to find out more

Hitler's War and the Germans
Marlis G. Steinert

The Conscience in Revolt: Portraits of the German Resistance 1933-45
Annedore Leber

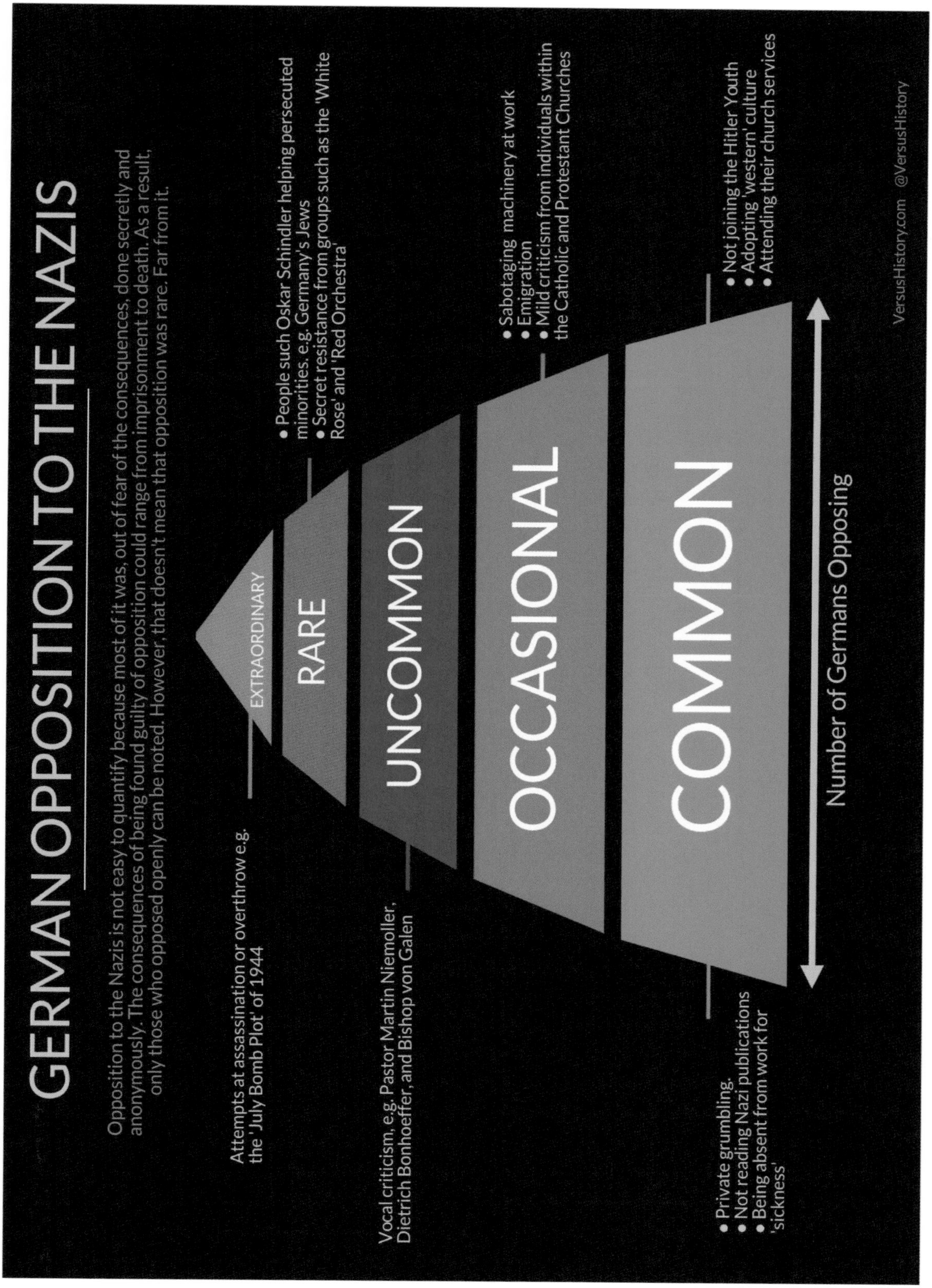
GERMAN OPPOSITION TO THE NAZIS
Opposition to the Nazis is not easy to quantify because most of it was, out of fear of the consequences, done secretly and anonymously. The consequences of being found guilty of opposition could range from imprisonment to death. As a result, only those who opposed openly can be noted. However, that doesn't mean that opposition was rare. Far from it.
EXTRAORDINARY
RARE
UNCOMMON
OCCASIONAL
COMMON
Attempts at assassination or overthrow e.g. the 'July Bomb Plot' of 1944
• People such Oskar Schindler helping persecuted minorities. e.g. Germany's Jews
• Secret resistance from groups such as the 'White Rose' and 'Red Orchestra'
Vocal criticism, e.g. Pastor Martin Niemoller, Dietrich Bonhoeffer, and Bishop von Galen
• Sabotaging machinery at work
• Emigration
• Mild criticism from individuals within the Catholic and Protestant Churches
• Private grumbling.
• Not reading Nazi publications
• Being absent from work for 'sickness'
• Not joining the Hitler Youth
• Adopting 'western' culture
• Attending their church services
Number of Germans Opposing
VersusHistory.com @VersusHistory

1933-45
foreign policy

Aiming abroad

Overview

In his first speech as chancellor of Germany in February 1933, Hitler lamented "The appalling fate that has dogged us since November 1918". In these few words, he immediately tied the problems of Germany to a foreign policy 'betrayal' – the signing of the Armistice that ended World War One – while simultaneously creating an apparent truism: that the successful future of *his* Germany required an *undoing* of this foreign policy betrayal. Consequently, the Third Reich, as Hitler envisioned it, would only truly come into existence by restoring Germany to its natural position as a dominant force in world foreign policy. This 'restoration' would be accomplished once Bolshevism and the Treaty of Versailles had been destroyed, Lebensraum in the east had been created, and a Greater Germany established beyond its current borders. In order to achieve any of these aims, war was to be expected.

Significance

The significance of Hitler's foreign policy aims, depends very much upon whether one believes them or not! Historians have long debated over whether Hitler had a 'blueprint' that he followed in his foreign policy – a viewpoint championed by the eminent Hugh Trevor Roper – or merely took opportunities where he saw them, piecemeal and ad hoc – the belief of the equally eminent A.J.P. Taylor. Perhaps the importance of Hitler's aims lies less in either of these two arguments, and more in what they would mean when carried out: ultimately, each and every one of these aims would, if challenged when being put into practice, lead to conflict. If successful, some would lead to murder and worse.

Historiography

"... Hitler's war aims are written large and clear in the documents of his reign. They are...different from the aims which have sometimes been ascribed to him by historians who regard him as a mere power-loving opportunist."

Hugh Trevor Roper
Hitler's War Aims (chapter in Aspects of the Third Reich)

Where to find out more

Hitler's War Aims
Norman Rich

Hitler's Plans for Global Domination
Jochen Thies

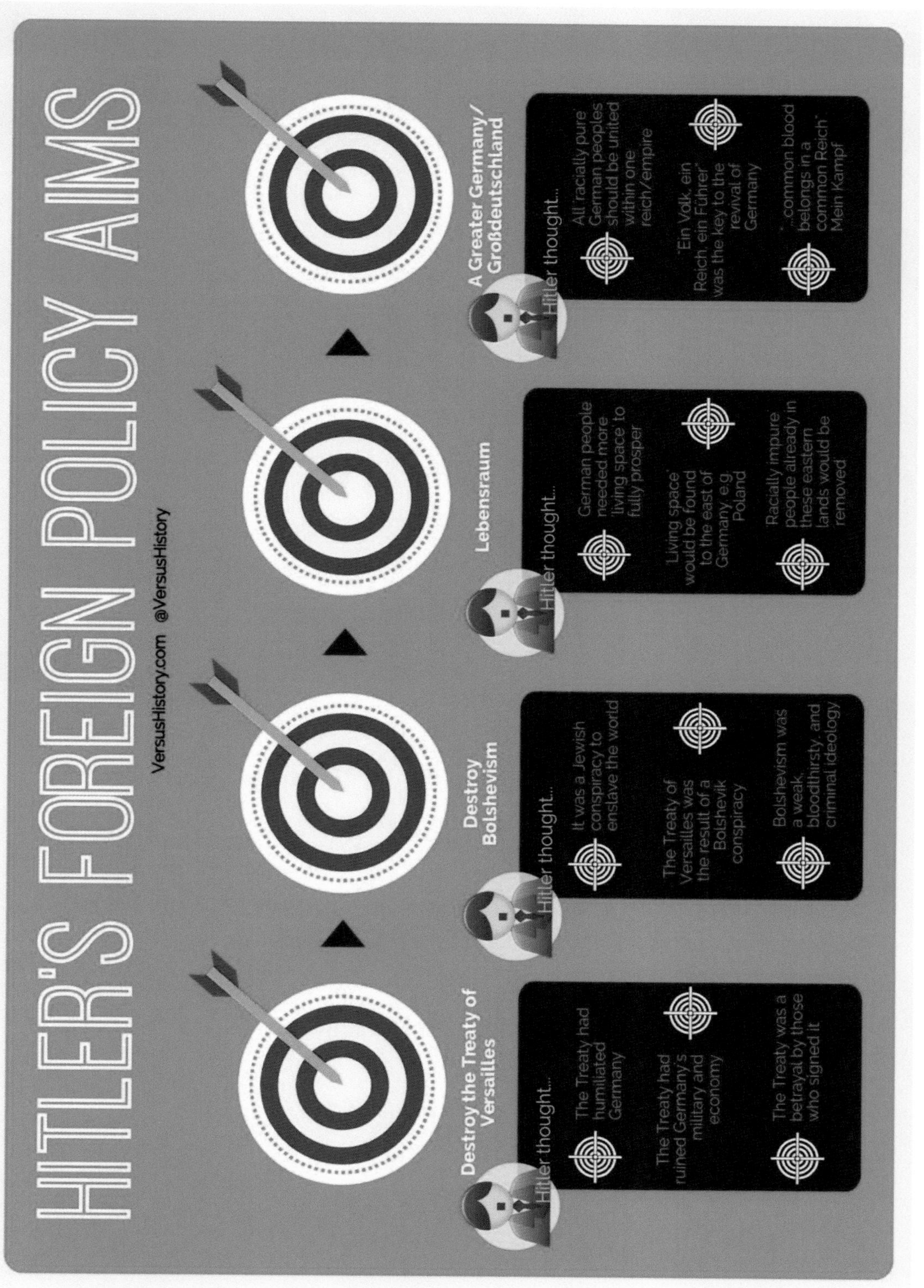
HITLER'S FOREIGN POLICY AIMS
VersusHistory.com @VersusHistory
Destroy the Treaty of Versailles
Hitler thought...
The Treaty had humiliated Germany
The Treaty had ruined Germany's military and economy
The Treaty was a betrayal by those who signed it
Destroy Bolshevism
Hitler thought...
It was a Jewish conspiracy to enslave the world
The Treaty of Versailles was the result of a Bolshevik conspiracy
Bolshevism was a weak, bloodthirsty, and criminal ideology
Lebensraum
Hitler thought...
German people needed more 'living space' to fully prosper
'Living space' would be found to the east of Germany, e.g. Poland
Racially impure people already in these eastern lands would be removed
A Greater Germany/ Großdeutschland
Hitler thought...
All 'racially pure' German peoples should be united within one reich/empire
"Ein Volk, ein Reich, ein Führer" was the key to the revival of Germany
"...common blood belongs in a common Reich" Mein Kampf

Hitler's 'step count'

Overview

As stated elsewhere in this book, Hitler's foreign policy was driven by some very clear engines: *lebensraum,* creating a *Greater Germany*, tearing up the Treaty of Versailles and such. Even a cursory review of the period 1933-39 would seem to suggest that it was, at least for Hitler, a roaring success – having seen almost every one of his foreign actions – some would say 'gambles' – result in success. When Hitler became chancellor, Germany was, militarily-speaking, a fallen giant. Within just six years, this European weakling would dominate Europe. In 1933, Hitler withdrew Germany from the League of Nations and, from this point onwards, we can trace an escalating series of steps that defied foreign treaties – particularly Versailles – broke the Covenant of the League of Nations, and ran roughshod over the policy of appeasement. He was even able to sign an agreement with Britain that secured Germany's right to break the Treaty of Versailles and rebuild Germany's navy! However, whether he meant all of his successes, is a matter of intense debate.

Significance

Whether a student in high school, university or beyond, it is a very particular challenge not to view Nazi foreign policy from 1933 onwards as a series of deliberate steps leading to an inevitable conclusion: World War Two. Of course, as we have said elsewhere in this book, that would be a backwards reading of history – seeing what *did* happen and assuming that the actors at the time knew all along what the actual outcomes of their actions were to be. While this may be *ahistorical*, it *can* be helpful when it comes to understanding the series of events – all of which are linked in some way, either by causation, correlation, or mere ideology – that took National Socialist Germany to war. Consequently, the infographic opposite was designed to simplify a very complex web of causation, motivation, and consequence into a more comprehensible series of actions and responses.

Historiography

"...there is not a scrap of evidence to support...the idea that Hitler had a distinctive "programme"."

Geoffrey Barraclough
Farewell to Hitler

Where to find out more

Hitler's Foreign Policy, 1933-1941: The Road to Global War
Christian Letz

Revenants of the German Empire
Sean Andrew Wempe

HITLER'S 12 STEPS TO WAR

@versushistory
versushistory.com

1

WITHDRAWAL FROM THE LEAGUE OF NATIONS, OCTOBER 1933

After western powers refused to accept military parity with Germany at the Disarmament Conference in February, Hitler withdraws Germany from the League.

2

SAAR PLEBISCITE, JANUARY 1935

The former German territory taken as a League of Nations mandate, voted for reunification with Germany in a referendum. An early success for Hitler's foreign policy.

3

REARMAMENT, 16TH MARCH 1935

Hitler announces rearmament - a public breaking of Versailles. GB, France and Italy ally in the Stresa Front to oppose any further breaking of the Treaty of Versailles. Within months the agreement collapses after Italy invades Abyssinia.

4

CONSCRIPTION, 16TH MARCH 1935

Hitler also announces the reintroduction of conscription - a further breaking of the Treaty of Versailles.

5

ANGLO-GERMAN NAVAL AGREEMENT, 18TH JUNE 1935

Britain makes an agreement with Germany whereby the tonnage of the Germany navy would never exceed 35% that of Britain's. This was in complete contravention of the naval limits placed on Germany by Versailles. GB saw it as an opportunity to limit German expansion. Hitler saw it as a beginning...

6

REMILITARISING THE RHINELAND. MARCH 7TH 1936

Hitler orders 19 infantry battalions into the Rhineland in direct contravention of Articles 42 & 43 of Versailles. There is no practical Allied response. The balance of power begins to shift in Germany's favour.

7

ANTI-COMINTERN PACT WITH JAPAN, NOVEMBER 25TH 1936

Hitler signs an agreement with Japan to counter the spread of communism, particularly from Russia. In 1937, this agreement would expand to include Italy.

8

'ANSCHLUSS' WITH AUSTRIA 12 MARCH, 1938

Hitler marches German troops into Austria and claims the state as part of Germany. This is arguably the first step in the creation of Hitler's 'Greater Germany'. There is little in the way of an Allied response.

9

MUNICH AGREEMENT, SEPTEMBER 1938

Hitler meets British PM Chamberlain whence it is agreed that Germany can 'have' part of Czechoslovakia called Sudetenland.

10

GERMANY TAKES THE REST OF CZECHOSLOVAKIA, MARCH 1939

Thus demonstrating to the allies that the policy of appeasement would never succeed.

11

NAZI-SOVIET PACT, AUGUST 1939

Hitler signs a neutrality agreement with Stalin as a prelude to his invasion of Poland.

12

HITLER INVADES POLAND, SEPTEMBER 1ST 1939

German forces invade from the north, south and west. On the 17th, Soviet forces invaded from the east. World War Two had started.

A recipe for disaster

Overview

After the devastation of World War One there was a collective will among many nations that it was an experience that should never again be repeated. The League of Nations was thus born out of the Paris Peace Conference and was 'baked' into the Treaty of Versailles: its first twenty-six clauses dealt with the League's establishment and was known as *The Covenant of the League of Nations*. Article X of this *Covenant* dealt with the need for collective security of member nations against the potential threat of territorial expansion and military aggression. Germany was only allowed to join the League in 1926. Upon coming to power, Hitler promptly withdrew Germany's membership and set about rearmament, territorial expansion and military aggression. At no point were the member nations of the League inclined to challenge him in any meaningful way.

Significance

History is not monocausal – World War Two was made manifest due to a complex mix of structural and circumstantial eventualities intricately woven with individual action and collective ambition. Having said this, one of the more significant contributors to Hitler's confidence in pursuing his belligerent expansion and military conquest, was the failure of the League of Nations to discourage or prevent it. Time and time again, the League failed to adequately censure nations for their aggression (see Japan in Manchuria and Italy in Abyssinia). Some argue that the League's failures to deal effectively with belligerents in the 1930's was doubly worse because it actually *encouraged* Hitler to carry out his transgressional foreign policy.

Historiography

"The human will will continue to seek escape from the logical consequences of realism in the vision of an international order which, as soon as it crystallizes itself into concrete political form, becomes tainted with self-interest and hypocrisy, and once more be attacked with the instruments of realism."

E.H. Carr
The Twenty Year Crisis

Where to find out more

The League of Nations at Work (documentary)
UN Audiovisual Library

People's Century – 1919: Lost Peace
PBS

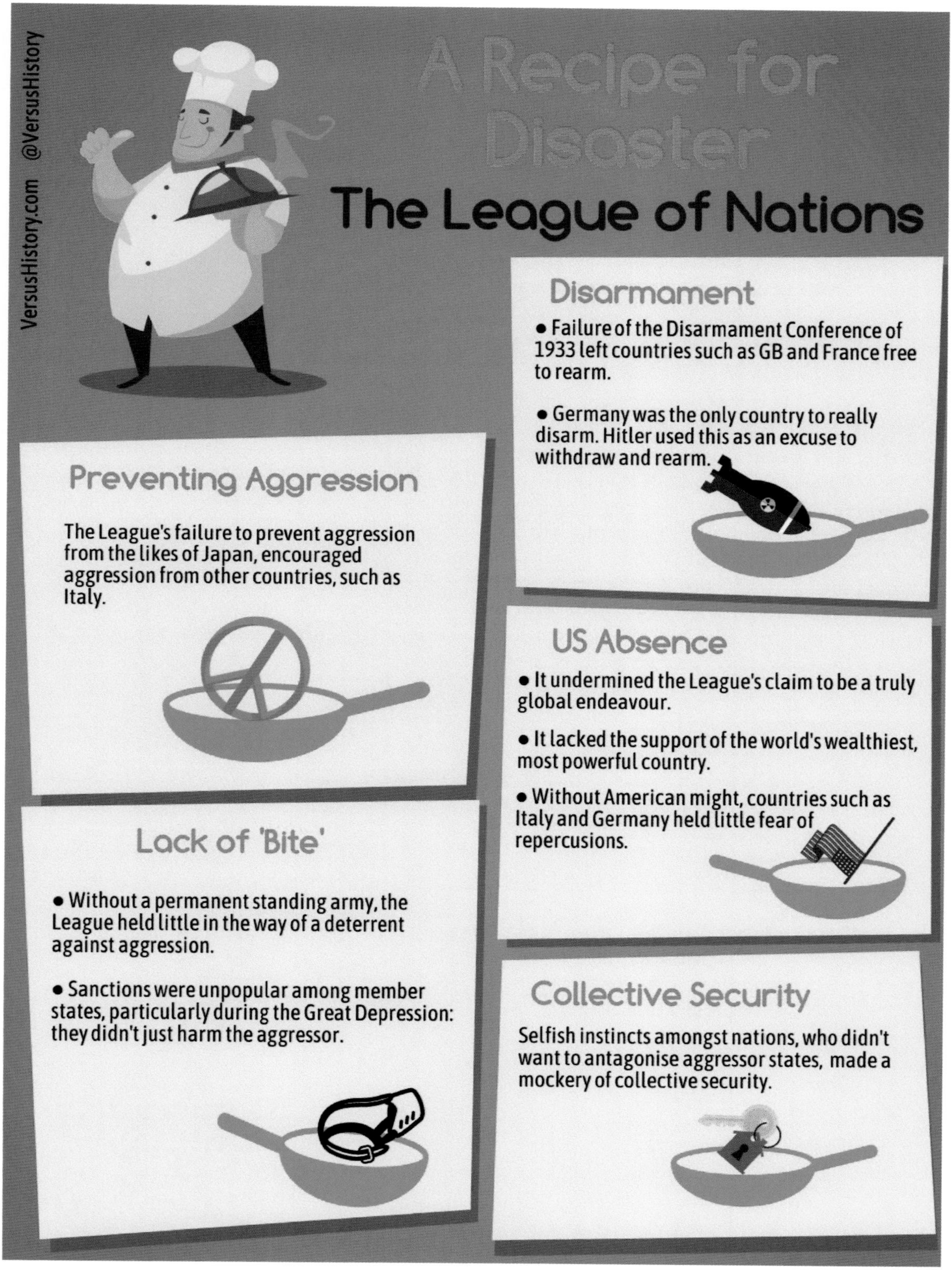
VersusHistory.com @VersusHistory
A Recipe for Disaster
The League of Nations
Disarmament
• Failure of the Disarmament Conference of 1933 left countries such as GB and France free to rearm.
• Germany was the only country to really disarm. Hitler used this as an excuse to withdraw and rearm.
Preventing Aggression
The League's failure to prevent aggression from the likes of Japan, encouraged aggression from other countries, such as Italy.
US Absence
• It undermined the League's claim to be a truly global endeavour.
• It lacked the support of the world's wealthiest, most powerful country.
• Without American might, countries such as Italy and Germany held little fear of repercusions.
Lack of 'Bite'
• Without a permanent standing army, the League held little in the way of a deterrent against aggression.
• Sanctions were unpopular among member states, particularly during the Great Depression: they didn't just harm the aggressor.
Collective Security
Selfish instincts amongst nations, who didn't want to antagonise aggressor states, made a mockery of collective security.

Lethal weapons: killing Versailles

Overview

The Treaty of Versailles eviscerated Germany's armed forces and with it a proud tradition of militarism dating back centuries. Most of the nationalist parties had made campaign promises to rearm Germany should they be voted into the Reichstag, regardless that any and all attempts at rearmament would stand in direct contravention of the treaty. Although there had been small-scale and secret programmes of rebuilding the German armed forces, it was only when Hitler came to power that these efforts became large-scale and, after 1935, public. For the Nazis, rearmament was a way to accomplish a number of ambitions: restore German pride; help reduce unemployment; prepare for war. Other than a few weak public statements from countries such as Britain and France, there was no substantive consequences to German militarism until they invaded Poland in 1939.

Significance

On 14th October 1933, Hitler announced that Germany would remove itself simultaneously from the Disarmament Conference and the League of Nations. In a world being shaped by the traumas of the Great Depression, national self-interest ensured that no countries were willing to confront Germany in a manner that might dissuade them from rebuilding their armed forces. Rearmament took many German companies out of financial crisis, provided employment during the Great Depression, and enabled an expansionist German foreign policy. It also triggered an arms race with some European countries which, in turn, helped create the context for another war.

Historiography

"Nothing stood in Hitler's way to transform Germany into the ultimate police and military state. The military was at Hitler's disposal for the implementation of his ideology brought about through war and violence."

Jason Ranke

The Anglo-American Press and the 'Secret' Rearmament of Hitler's Germany, 1933 to 1935

Where to find out more

German Rearmament and the West, 1932-1933
Edward W. Bennett

The Wages of Destruction
Adam Tooze

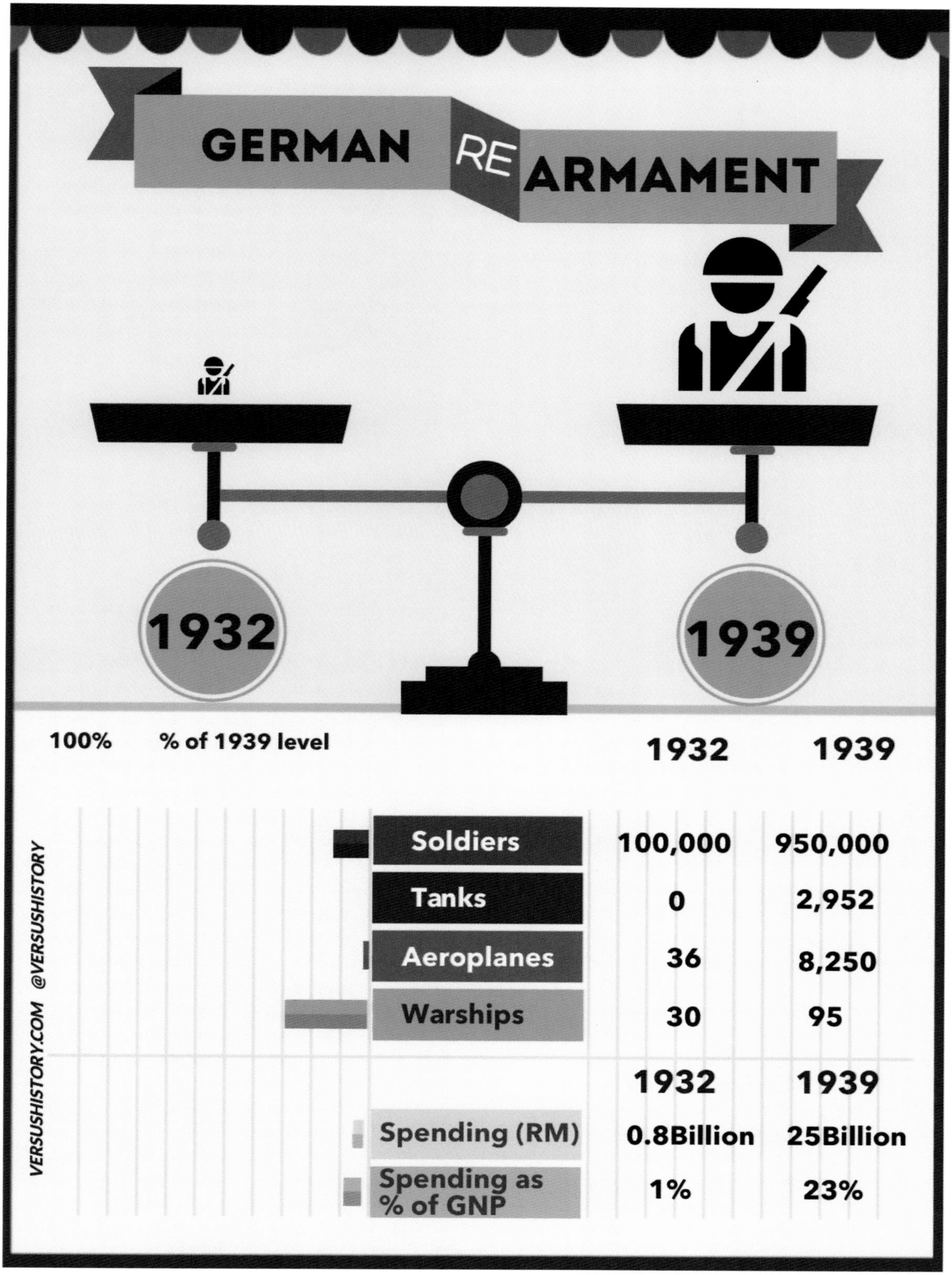
GERMAN RE ARMAMENT
1932
1939
100%
% of 1939 level
1932
1939
Soldiers
100,000
950,000
Tanks
0
2,952
Aeroplanes
36
8,250
Warships
30
95
1932
1939
Spending (RM)
0.8Billion
25Billion
Spending as % of GNP
1%
23%
VERSUSHISTORY.COM @VERSUSHISTORY

Getting away with murder

Overview

On 3rd of September 1939, Britain and France declared war on Germany. The decision by the Allies to finally stand up to German expansionism was the culmination of a policy, driven primarily by Great Britain, of allowing Hitler to indulge his foreign policy desires in the 1930's. For a complex mixture of reasons, both Britain and France preferred not to confront Hitler's military and territorial expansion in the belief that, not only were some of his ambitions 'reasonable', but also that war was to be avoided if possible. From French weakness after the War, to the problems associated with the Great Depression which took such an economic and social toll on the world, to Britain's wish to avoid the kind of bloodshed experienced during 1914-18, time and time again, Hitler was allowed to contravene large sections of the Versailles settlement as well as international law.

Significance

When Hitler took control of Czechoslovakia in March 1939, after agreeing with British PM Neville Chamberlain in Munich that he would not do so, the policy of appeasement was revealed for what Churchill described it to be in October 1938 : "... a disaster of the first magnitude". Despite the rationale used to justify it, appeasement seemed not to reduce the chance of aggression but, ultimately, to encourage it. With every foreign policy gamble that paid off – from rearmament to taking the Sudetenland – Hitler felt emboldened by the lack of existential consequences. As a result, and according to many at the time and since, he merely kept doing as he pleased until somebody stood up to him. The only time this happened was on 3rd of September 1939 – 6 years after he became chancellor. By this time, Hitler and Nazi Germany were too strong to be challenged.

Historiography

"The peace settlement…came to be perceived by all (British) political parties and by the public… as unduly harsh… Hitler's rearmament… the remilitarization of the Rhineland… and the occupation of the Sudetenland were all significant attacks on the Versailles system which most groups in Britain had come to consider unworthy of defense."

Catherine Ann Cline
British Historians and the Treaty of Versailles

Where to find out more

Appeasing Hitler: Chamberlain, Churchill and the Road to War
Tim Bouverie

Munich 1938: Appeasement and World War II
David Faber

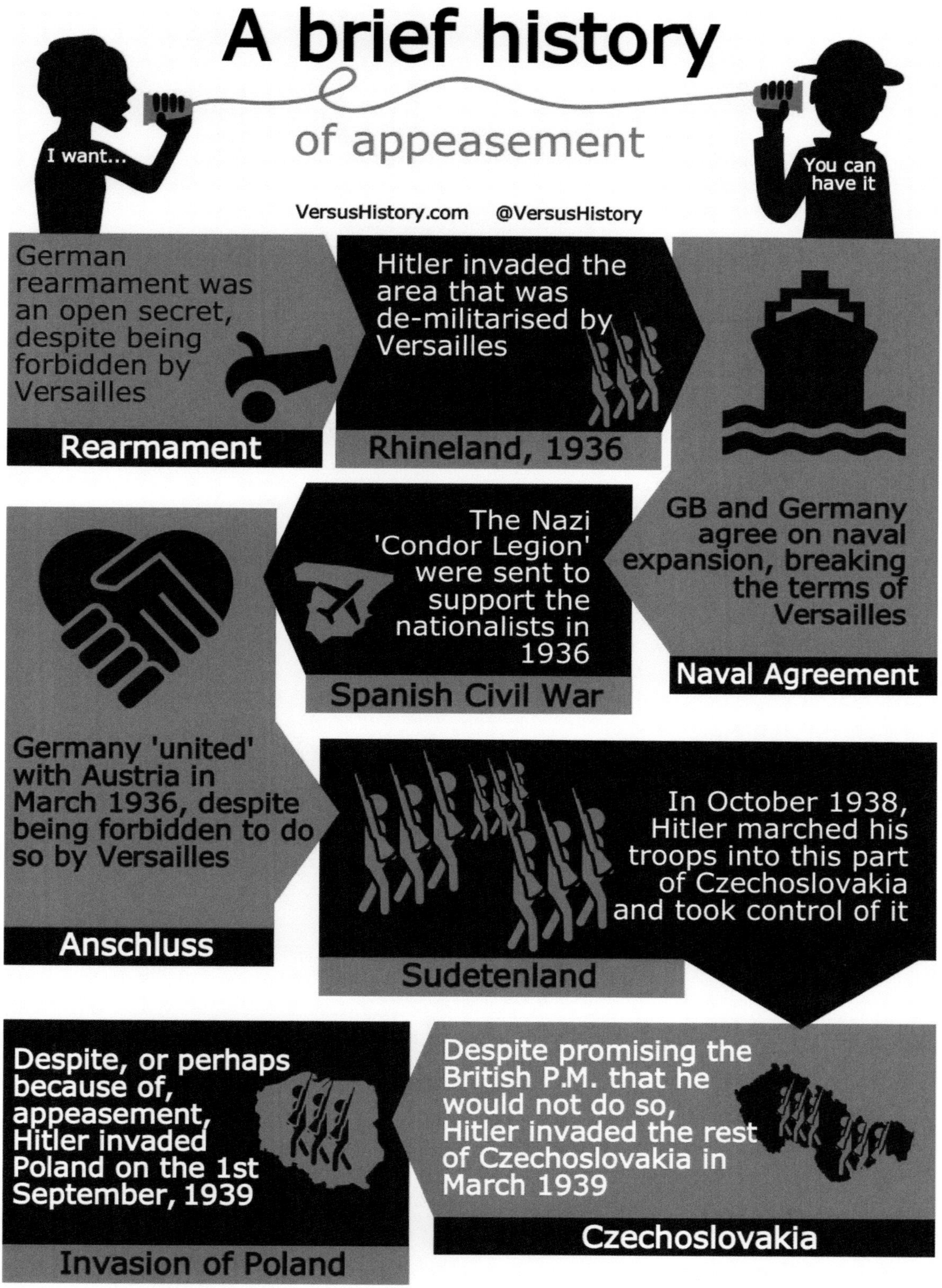
A brief history
of appeasement
I want...
You can have it
VersusHistory.com @VersusHistory
German rearmament was an open secret, despite being forbidden by Versailles
Rearmament
Hitler invaded the area that was de-militarised by Versailles
Rhineland, 1936
GB and Germany agree on naval expansion, breaking the terms of Versailles
Naval Agreement
The Nazi 'Condor Legion' were sent to support the nationalists in 1936
Spanish Civil War
Germany 'united' with Austria in March 1936, despite being forbidden to do so by Versailles
Anschluss
In October 1938, Hitler marched his troops into this part of Czechoslovakia and took control of it
Sudetenland
Despite promising the British P.M. that he would not do so, Hitler invaded the rest of Czechoslovakia in March 1939
Czechoslovakia
Despite, or perhaps because of, appeasement, Hitler invaded Poland on the 1st September, 1939
Invasion of Poland

A matter of perspective

Overview

The obvious question that must be asked by students of history is his: "If the policy of appeasement seems so unwise to us, why was it followed at all?". The answer is complex but it must be bound up with the equally obvious: "It mustn't have seemed unwise at the time; perhaps it wasn't as unwise as we seem to think it". As the broad unwillingness of the League of Nations to act against the belligerence of Italy, Japan, and Germany during the 1930's attests, national self-interest clearly trumped collective action. The multi-layered concerns of Britain and France, ranging from the possible spread of communism from Soviet Russia, to the protection of the British Empire in the event of a global conflict, as well as the effects of the Great Depression and the sympathy many politicians in Britain had for a Germany ruined by Versailles, meant that appeasement of Germany was the only real tool available at the time to meet their complex needs.

Significance

Looking back on history from our vantage point, it is easy to see the policy of appeasement – that of allowing Hitler to accomplish his goals provided they did not appear too *unreasonable* – as fundamentally flawed or profoundly unwise. This is because we, as students of history, know where this policy helped lead: to World War Two. However, this view is in itself fundamentally flawed – because we are indulging in the 'sin' of reading history *backwards;* we are judging actions based upon the knowledge of where those actions led – which was not an insight people at the time had the privilege of using. Consequently, the policy of appeasement needs to be viewed – as far as is possible – through contemporaneous eyes. In this manner, we can conduct a more honest appraisal of the policy.

Historiography

"... men confronted with real problems, doing their best in the circumstances of their time."

A.J.P. Taylor
The Origins of the Second World War

Where to find out more

Neville Chamberlain, Appeasement and the British Road to War
Frank McDonough

Europe and the Czechs
Shiela Grant Duff

Positive ••• vs ••• Negative
APPEASEMENT
Europe was 'saved from war'. Chamberlain thought it brought: "Peace for our time"
WAR
It encouraged Hitler: he thought GB & France would not use force to oppose him
It gave Britain and France time to prepare for war
SELF-INTEREST
Czechoslovakia was abandoned, giving Hitler his first step towards lebensraum
Germany would remain a cooperative 'buffer' against the spread of communism
COMMUNISM
Stalin felt excluded; he decided he couldn't trust GB and France. This pushed him into the Nazi-Soviet Pact
VersusHistory.com @VersusHistory

A marriage of convenience

Overview

On August 23rd, 1939 – just eight days before Hitler's war machine rolled into Poland – Germany's Foreign Minister, Joachim von Ribbentrop, met with his Soviet counterpart, Vyacheslav Molotov, in Moscow. At its core, the agreement that was arrived at by the two men was one of non-aggression – a reciprocal promise to respect each other's borders and spheres of influence. Despite its complexity, with secret protocols involving countries such as Latvia, Lithuania, and Finland, Hitler's primary goal was to receive assurances from Stalin that, should he move on Poland, Russia would not mobilise against Germany.

Significance

The neutrality inherent in the Nazi -Soviet Pact served both Hitler and Stalin well. Stalin was no fool, he was keenly aware of Hitler's very public hatred for the USSR and communism. He was also keenly aware of what could be gained from agreeing to neutrality: a delay of any war with Germany, land in Poland lost by Russia during World War One, and an insurance policy against the machinations of France and Germany, whom he didn't trust. For Hitler, and the fate of Europe, the pact was of profound importance: it gave Hitler a 'free pass' to invade Poland without Soviet repercussions, regain the 'Polish Corridor' and the port of Danzig - both lost at Versailles – and it acted as a deterrent against any British and French response, now that he was allied with Stalin. This last did not happen: two days after his invasion of Poland, Britain and France declared war on Germany, starting another world war.

Historiography

"... (the NS Pact) is normally associated with one of the darkest periods in modern diplomatic history...it is generally seen as a cautionary tale about ***realpolitik*** *– which led to disastrous miscalculations by Stalin as well as Hitler."*

David Wedgwood Benn
Russian historians defend the Molotov–Ribbentrop Pact

Where to find out more

The Devil's Alliance: Hitler's Pact with Stalin, 1939-41
Roger Moorhouse

Stalin: Waiting for Hitler, 1929-41
Stephen Kotkin

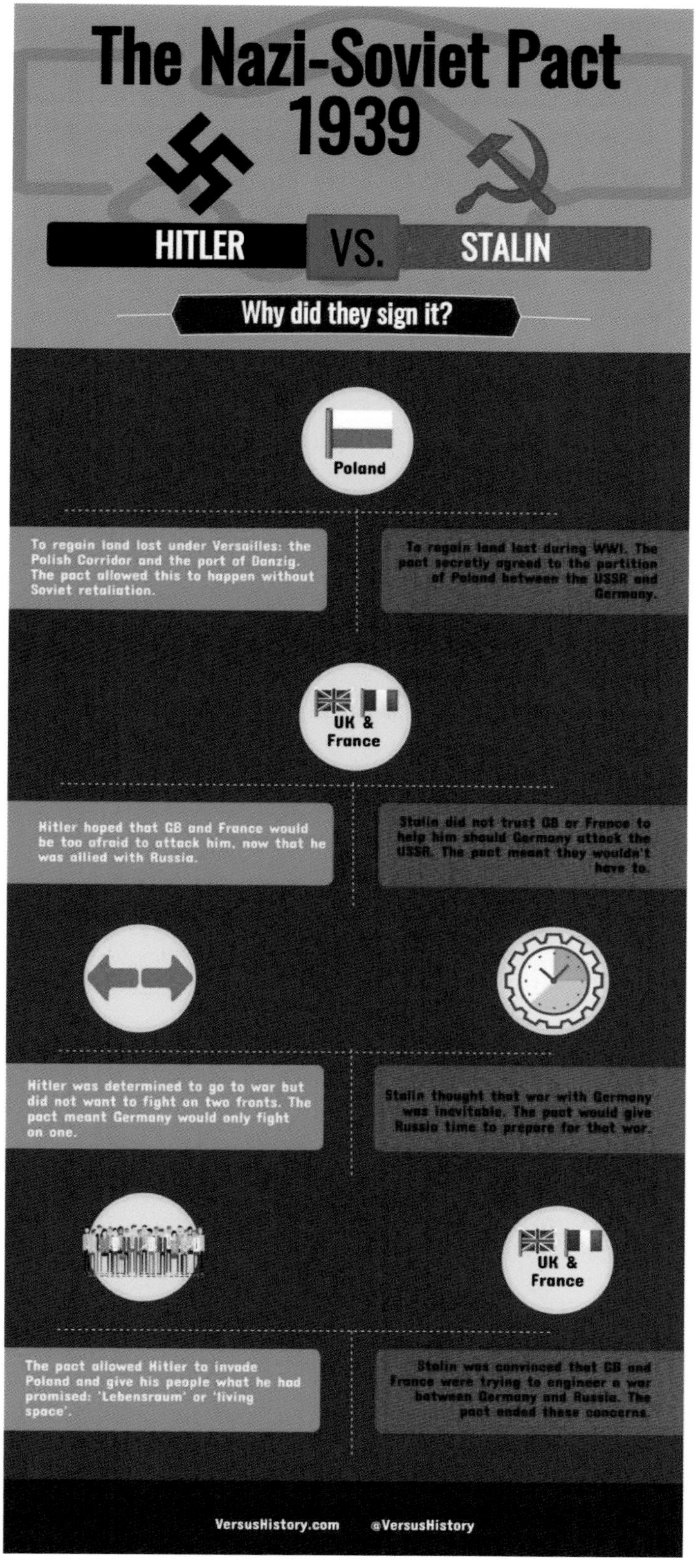
The Nazi-Soviet Pact
1939
HITLER
VS.
STALIN
Why did they sign it?
Poland
To regain land lost under Versailles: the Polish Corridor and the port of Danzig. The pact allowed this to happen without Soviet retaliation.
To regain land lost during WWI. The pact secretly agreed to the partition of Poland between the USSR and Germany.
UK & France
Hitler hoped that GB and France would be too afraid to attack him, now that he was allied with Russia.
Stalin did not trust GB or France to help him should Germany attack the USSR. The pact meant they wouldn't have to.
Hitler was determined to go to war but did not want to fight on two fronts. The pact meant Germany would only fight on one.
Stalin thought that war with Germany was inevitable. The pact would give Russia time to prepare for that war.
UK & France
The pact allowed Hitler to invade Poland and give his people what he had promised: 'Lebensraum' or 'living space'.
Stalin was convinced that GB and France were trying to engineer a war between Germany and Russia. The pact ended these concerns.
VersusHistory.com
@VersusHistory

Perfect timing

Overview

From the moment Hitler withdrew Germany from the League of Nations in 1933, to his invasion of Poland in September 1939, his foreign policy record was stunning. Barely a false step was made between 1933-1939, in which time the Nazi regime engineered a series of staggering triumphs that, when viewed from our vantage point in history, appear to be destined to lead to a Second World War. However, this is clearly not an honest way of evaluating history.

Significance

Looking back at Hitler's foreign policy successes in the 1930's it is easy to view them as an escalating series of steps, pre-planned and orchestrated by a master tactician moving towards an ultimate goal. By and large, this is not the correct way to view his foreign policy. Hitler was very much an opportunist during the 1930's, inasmuch as, though he had goals to achieve, it was usually only when an opportunity presented itself, or when resistance was weak, that he pushed for what he wanted. His territorial expansion and rearmament were underpinned by the policy of *appeasement* followed by Britain and France. For example, when Hitler decided to remilitarise the Rhineland in 1936, he did so because he felt that the situation in Europe allowed for it: Locarno looked to be dying and the French, building up the Maginot line, were looking to defend, not attack; the League was focused on Italy in Abyssinia. Even the former PM, Lloyd George, addressing the British House of Commons, stated that Hitler was justified in remilitarising the territory. When Hitler sent his troops in, they marched with the full understanding that any offensive French resistance should be met with a German U-turn. When no resistance was forthcoming, Hitler felt emboldened into further action.

Historiography

"... in March 1936 the two Western democracies, were given their last chance to halt, without the risk of a serious war, the rise of a militarized, aggressive, totalitarian Germany and...bring the Nazi dictator and his regime tumbling down. They let the chance slip."

William L. Shirer
The Rise and Fall of the Third Reich

Where to find out more

What Hitler Knew: The Battle for Information in Nazi Foreign Policy
Zachary Shore

Churchill, Hitler, and "The Unnecessary War"
Patrick J. Buchanan

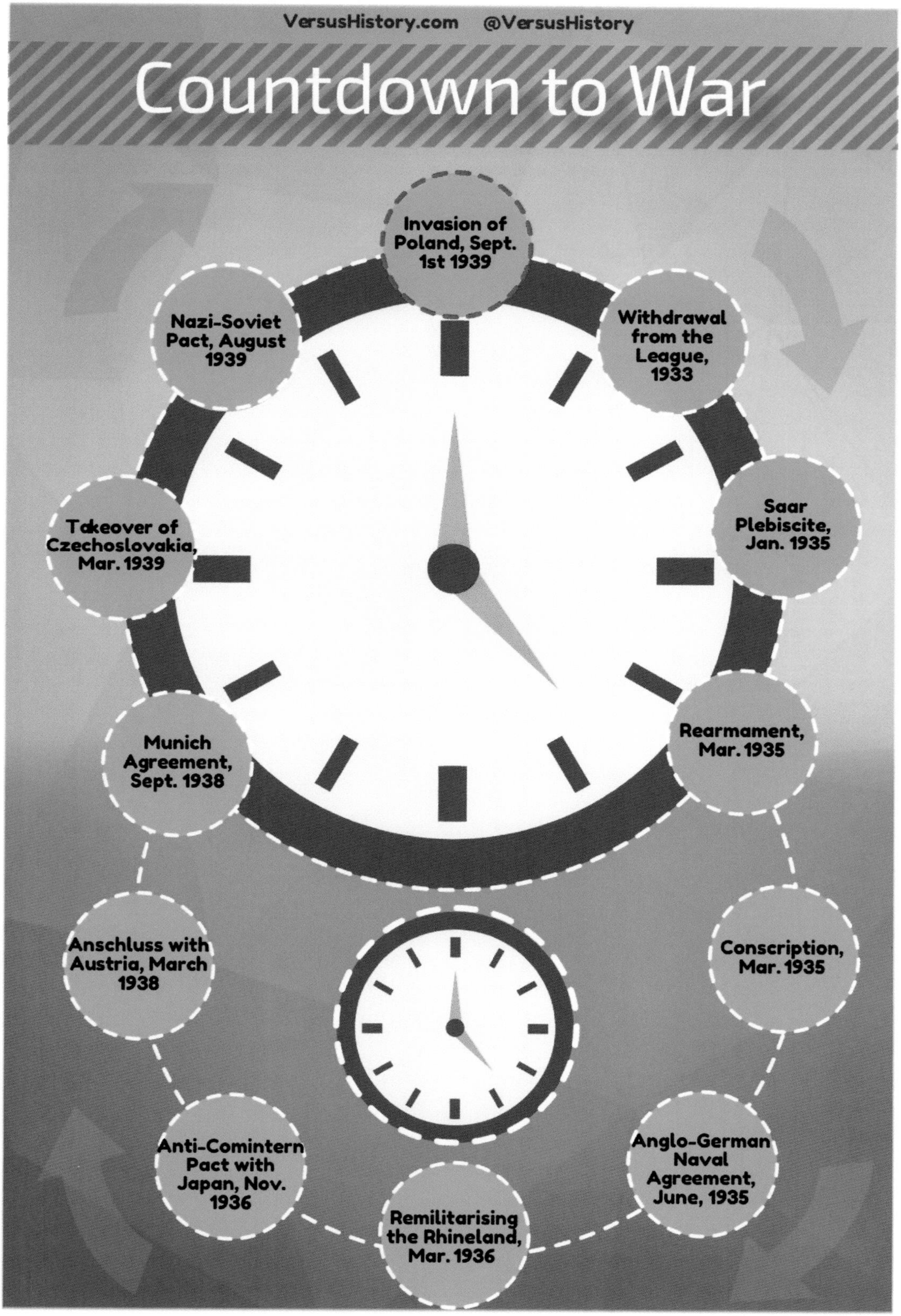
VersusHistory.com @VersusHistory
Countdown to War
Invasion of Poland, Sept. 1st 1939
Withdrawal from the League, 1933
Saar Plebiscite, Jan. 1935
Rearmament, Mar. 1935
Conscription, Mar. 1935
Anglo-German Naval Agreement, June, 1935
Remilitarising the Rhineland, Mar. 1936
Anti-Comintern Pact with Japan, Nov. 1936
Anschluss with Austria, March 1938
Munich Agreement, Sept. 1938
Takeover of Czechoslovakia, Mar. 1939
Nazi-Soviet Pact, August 1939

The Reich's report

Overview

It is no exaggeration to say that from his inauguration in 1933 to the outbreak of World War Two in 1939, Hitler's foreign policy was impressively successful. Action after action, decision after decision, appeared to gain almost precisely what he set out to for. Whether out of foreign policy acumen, sheer brazenness, or pure luck, time after time Hitler was able to do what he wanted and take what he desired. More than this, his actions, many of which were in direct contravention of the Versailles settlement, the League of Nations, and signed international agreements, went largely unchallenged by both the League and the great powers of Europe. Even *before* his armies invaded Poland on 1st September 1939, Hitler had already succeeded beyond even his own expectations.

Significance

AJP Taylor considered Hitler's foreign policy achievements during this period a result of opportunism and audacity. He claimed that Hitler had no overarching plan for a European war of destruction but was 'allowed' to get away with so much that he felt confident that neither Britain nor France would intervene when he invaded Poland. Hugh Trevor-Roper, on the other hand, felt that Hitler was carrying out a *Stufenplan* – staged plan – premeditated and willed into existence; carried out by his Foreign Ministers Konstantin von Neurath and Joachim von Ribbentrop. Regardless of the truth of the matter (which was probably a mix of the two: an opportunism that helped Hitler accomplish overarching goals) by the time Hitler Britain declared war on Germany on 3rd September 1939, Hitler's Europe was already well on the way to being a reality.

Historiography

"His aim was… the overthrow of the existing European order; his method was patience. Despite his bluster and violent talk, he was a master in the game of waiting. He never made a frontal attack on a prepared position - At least never until his judgment had been corrupted by easy victories."

A.J.P. Taylor
The Origins of the Second World War

Where to find out more

From Kaiserreich to Third Reich: Elements of Continuity in German History, 1871-1945
Fritz Fischer

Hitler's Foreign Policy 1933 - 1939: The Road to World War II
Gerhard L. Weinberg

Hitler's Foreign Policy
1933-39
Report Card
Rearmed without repercussions
Occupied the Rhineland
Tested Luftwaffe in Spain
Appeasement worked in his favour
GB convinced he only wanted peace
Was not bound by the League
Japan supported him against USSR
Military alliance with Italy
99% of Austria voted for Anschluss
Began building his 'Greater Germany'
Gained resources in Sudetenland
Took lebensraum in Czechoslovakia
USSR allowed his invasion of Poland
VersusHistory.com @VersusHistory

A flash in the panzer

Overview

When Hitler's troops invaded Poland on 1st September 1939, they were beginning a campaign of near-unbroken military success that would last until mid-1941. In a series of short 'lightning bursts', the Wehrmacht attacked country after country in Europe. From Poland to Denmark, Belgium to France, Hitler's armies smashed through frontlines using 'narrow' columns of infantry, tanks, and mobile artillery, all the while being supported from the air by the Luftwaffe. Once inside enemy territory, German forces would encircle their opponents and terrorise the interior of each country. This style of warfare was known as *Blitzkrieg*, or *Lightning War*, because of its rapid, often surprising, onset and deadly destruction.

Significance

The Blitzkrieg tactic was largely responsible for the staggering successes of the Nazi war machine in the early years of the war. Within just nine months, Hitler had taken control of much of Europe, including France. The British Expeditionary Force (BEF) was ignominiously proved to be no match for either the tactic or the vastly superior-in-numbers German military, evacuated, as it had to be, from the beaches of Dunkirk. The significance of these early successes should not be underestimated – it had achieved in less than a year what the Kaiser, in four years of staggering losses, could not do: conquer France and subdue the continent. One of the big differences between the Kaiser's military and that of Hitler was that, while both relied on speed for their attacks, only one had the technology to achieve it. The Blitzkrieg brought the war to the shores of the English Channel; Britain had little option but to defend itself. It would also, within a year, be brought to bear in the east against the USSR.

Historiography

"Hitler's 'concept of Blitzkrieg' dominates the political and military history of Germany's strategy in the Second World War."

Tobias Jersak

Blitzkrieg Revisited: A New Look at Nazi War and Extermination Planning

Where to find out more

The Blitzkrieg Legend: The 1940 Campaign in the West
James Holland

The Fall of France: The Nazi Invasion of 1940
Julian Jackson

NAZI BLITZKRIEG

HITLER'S 'LIGHTNING WAR'

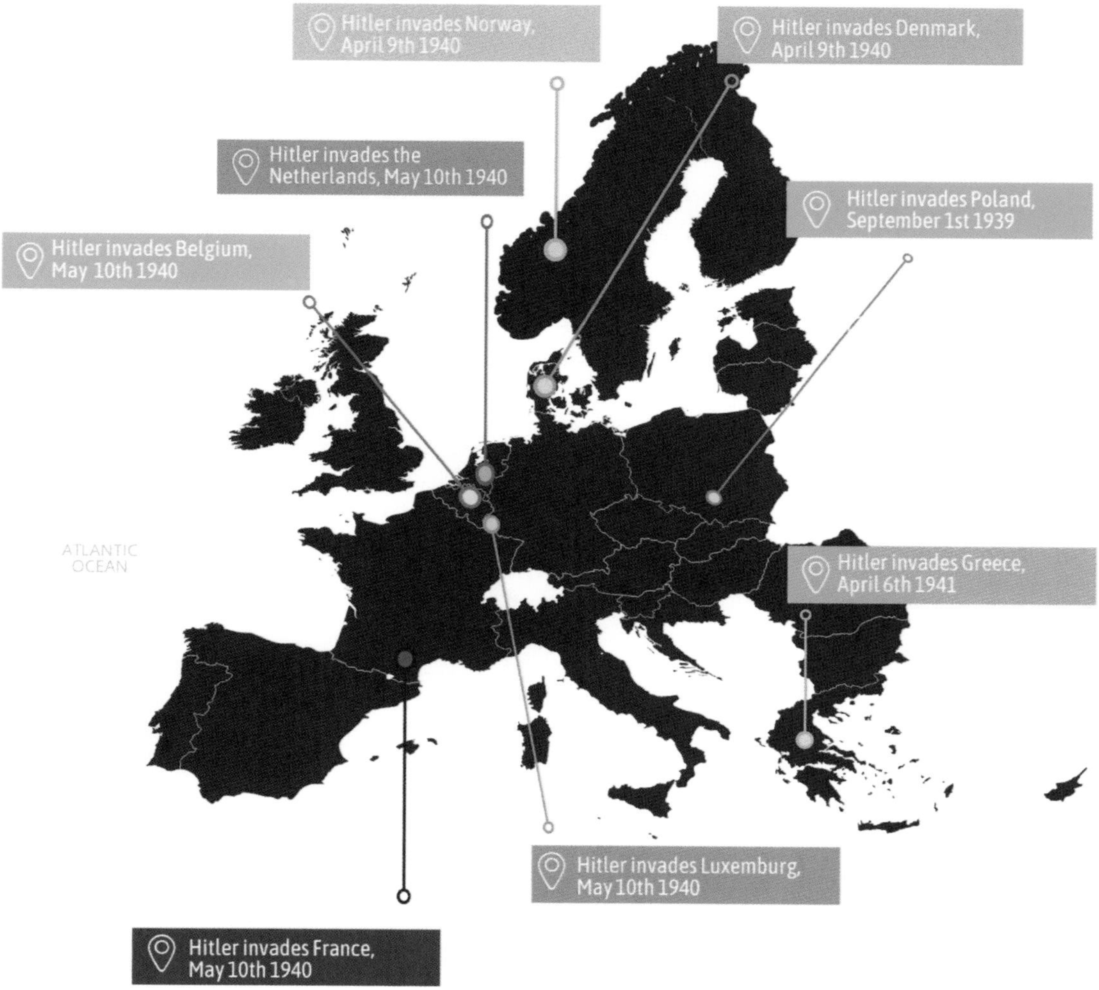

VersusHistory.com #VersusHistory @VersusHistory

The sky's the limit (for Hitler)

Overview

Right up until June 1940, Hitler was sure that Britain would sue for peace with Germany rather than risk an all-out conflict that he was certain they would lose. When the predicted peace treaty was not forthcoming, Hitler ordered plans to be drawn up for the invasion of Great Britain – codenamed 'Operation Sealion'. Many of his more experienced generals were doubtful of the success of such an enterprise – particularly fearing the might of the Royal Navy and the Royal Air Force. Hermann Göring, the head of Germany's Luftwaffe, however, was far more confident. He convinced Hitler that the first stage of any invasion would be an aerial assault on key RAF targets, particularly in the south and south east of England. And so, on 10th of July, the Luftwaffe began an ever-escalating series of attacks on British shipping in the English Channel. On 13th August, the main offensive of *Unternehmen Adlerangriff* – Operation Eagle Attack – began. For the next four months Britain's Royal Air Force came to the rescue against the onslaught, in what became known as the *Battle of Britain.*

Significance

The Royal Air Force Fighter Command, with two of the most advanced fighter plane designs in the world – the Spitfire and the Hurricane – took to the skies to defend against the Luftwaffe. Their ultimate victory, enabled by the 'Dowding System', the 'Chain Home System', rapid industrial production, and young men from all over the Commonwealth, dealt Hitler his first taste of defeat. It also helped convince the Americans – many of whom had felt Britain would be easy prey for Germany, and thus saw little point in supporting them militarily – that they were worthy of aid. The Battle of Britain weakened the Luftwaffe – some say fatally – and meant that Britain could live to fight another day, which they did on D-Day.

Historiography

"Adolf Hitler met his first defeat in eight years… (the Battle of Britain would) go down in history as a battle as important as Waterloo or Gettysburg."

Ralph Ingersoll
Report on England, November 1940

Where to find out more

The Battle of Britain: The Real Story (Documentary, BBC)
James Holland

The Most Dangerous Enemy
Stephen Bungay

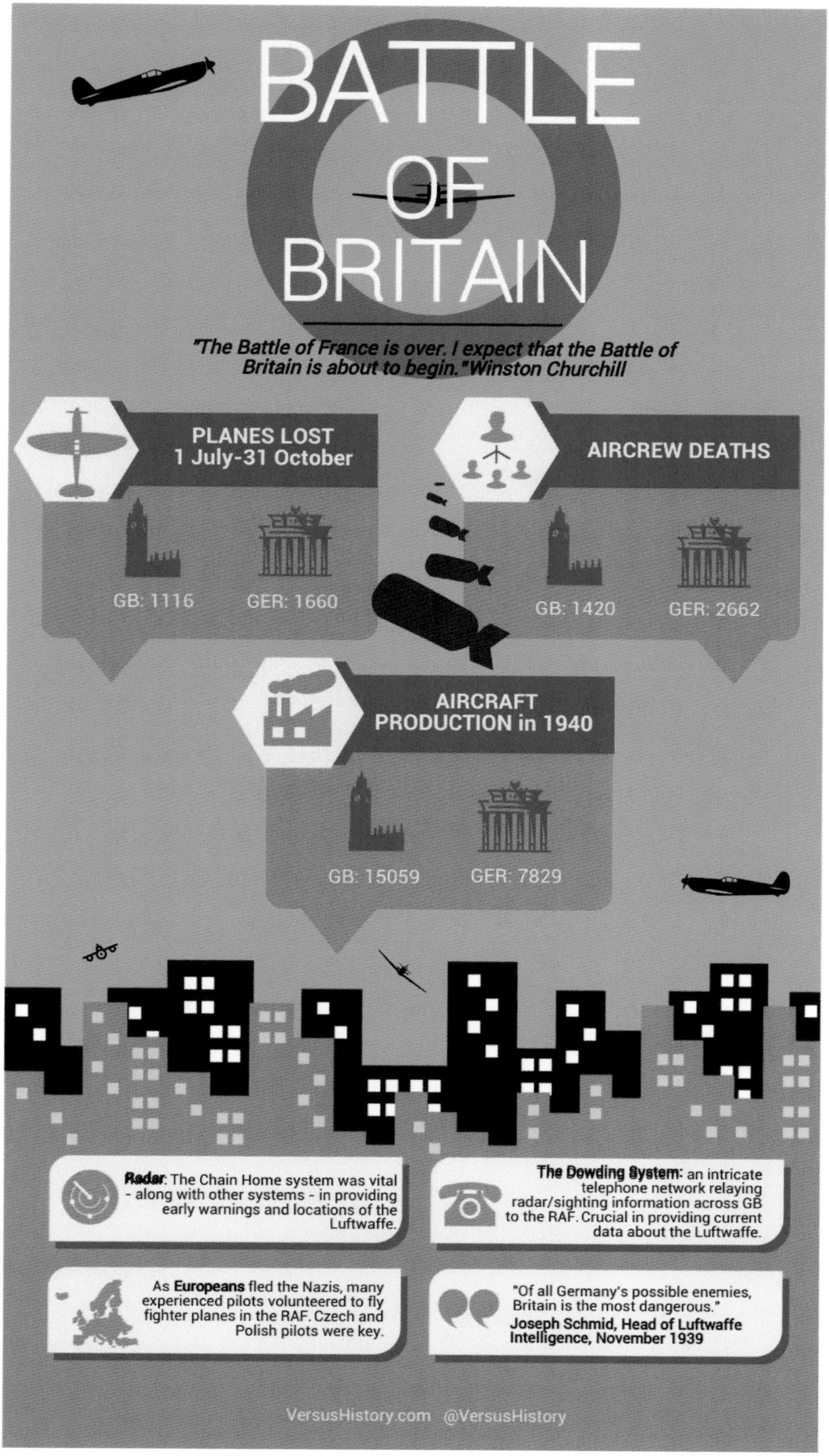
BATTLE OF BRITAIN
"The Battle of France is over. I expect that the Battle of Britain is about to begin." Winston Churchill
PLANES LOST 1 July-31 October
GB: 1116
GER: 1660
AIRCREW DEATHS
GB: 1420
GER: 2662
AIRCRAFT PRODUCTION in 1940
GB: 15059
GER: 7829
Radar: The Chain Home system was vital - along with other systems - in providing early warnings and locations of the Luftwaffe.
The Dowding System: an intricate telephone network relaying radar/sighting information across GB to the RAF. Crucial in providing current data about the Luftwaffe.
As Europeans fled the Nazis, many experienced pilots volunteered to fly fighter planes in the RAF. Czech and Polish pilots were key.
"Of all Germany's possible enemies, Britain is the most dangerous."
Joseph Schmid, Head of Luftwaffe Intelligence, November 1939
VersusHistory.com @VersusHistory

Russia: Hitler's fatal attraction

Overview

When Adolf Hitler ordered his Wehrmacht to attack the Soviet Union in June 1941, he was attempting to achieve something that Napoleon before him could not: to conquer the Russian people, the Russian landscape, and the Russian weather. He was also reneging on the non-aggression pact he had signed with Stalin in 1939. Hitler's hatred for the peoples in the east, of Bolshevism, and his need for so-called lebensraum for the German people, led him to underestimate, just as Napoleon had done in 1812, the people, the terrain, and the climate of Russia. By early December and 24 kilometres from Moscow, German troops caught sight of the Kremlin. However, this would be as close to it as they would ever get. The ferocious Russian winter arrived like an anvil and the Second Front in the east went from being a Nazi dream, to an unceasing nightmare for the Third Reich.

Significance

Hitler's decision to open a *Second Front* created a chasm between their operations in the west and those now in the east which could not be bridged, either by resources, equipment, or manpower. Operation Barbarossa divided the Wehrmacht in a way that, had it been temporary and successful, it may have endured; had it enjoyed the same success as the European Blitzkrieg in the early months of the war, then a different history of the war might have been written. As it was, Hitler's gamble – and it was that – led to the destruction of the myth of German invincibility. More than this, Russia's ultimate, though horrifically attritional, victory literally turned the direction of the Nazi war machine from expansion to contraction. It would also provide an opportunity for Stalin to realise his authoritarian vision for the Soviet domination of eastern Europe.

Historiography

"...the Russo-German war, a war that not only determined the outcome of the Second World War but defined the post-World War II world until the collapse of the USSR in 1991."

Leo J. Daugherty III

'Barbarossa' Revisited: The War on the Eastern Front, 1941–1945: A Survey of Recent Literature

Where to find out more

Operation Barbarossa: The German Invasion of Soviet Russia
Robert Kirchubel

Barbarossa: Reframing Hitler's Invasion of Stalin's Soviet Empire
Frank Ellis

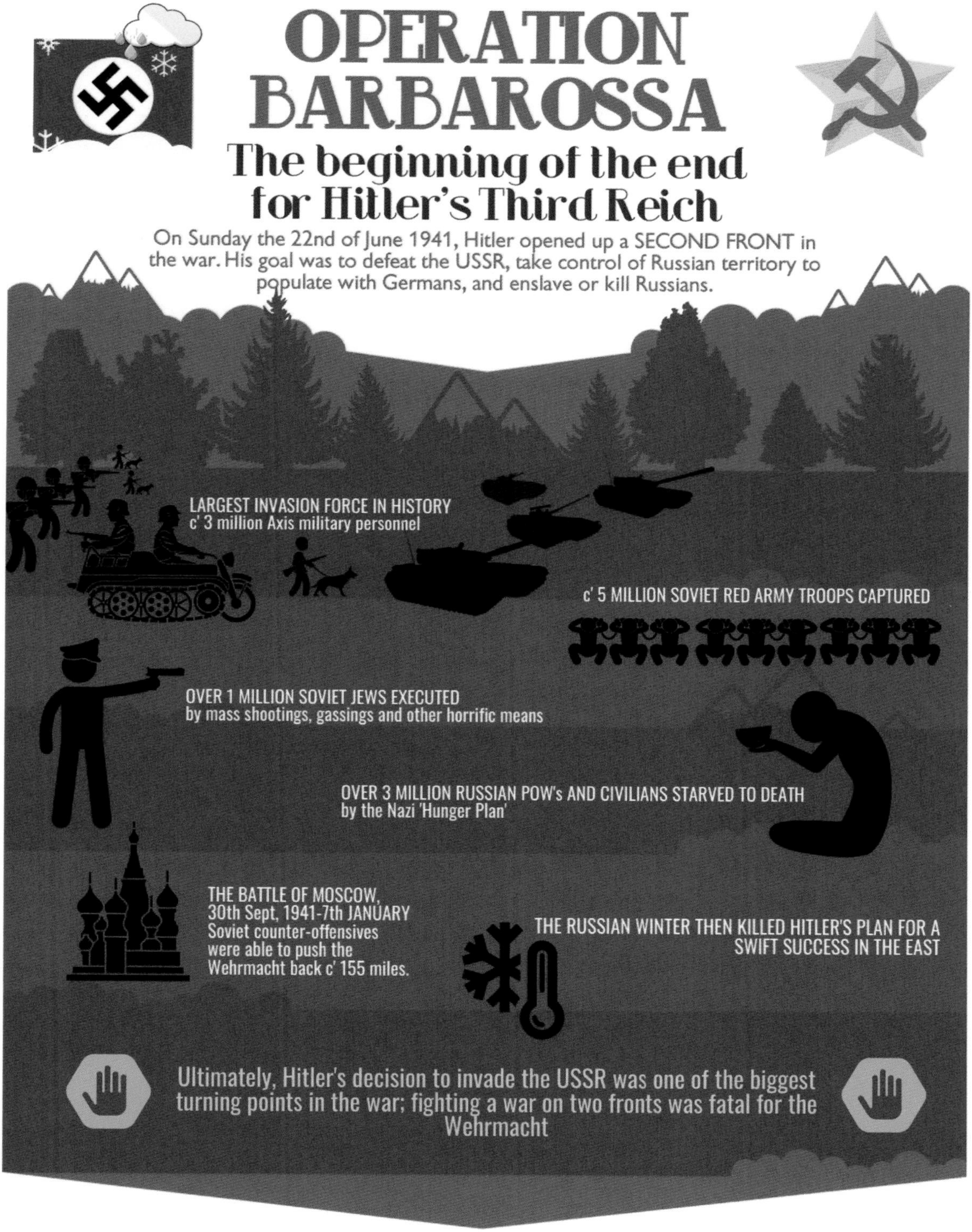

VersusHistory.com
@VersusHistory

6 June 1944: sandstorm

Overview

Long before the sun had risen above the English Channel on 6th June, 18,000 American and British paratroopers were deploying inland beyond the beaches of Normandy. Just a few hours after their scattered landings, Operation Neptune – one of the largest amphibious military offensives in history – was launched against the monstrously fortified German defences which lined the north-west coast of France. Close to 160,000 British, Canadian, and American forces landed on five beaches, ultimately opening the long-awaited *Second Front* against a Germany which was already retreating from the Soviet Red Army in the east.

Significance

Operation Overlord was the largest, air, sea and land operation in military history. Its goal was to punch a hole in the German defences in western Europe, providing an entry point for the Allies to begin pushing the Wehrmacht back to Berlin. Although the *D-Day landings* were successful, there were tragic losses of life as the German military stubbornly resisted the onslaught. Additionally, *D-Day* was only the beginning. Over the next three months, the Allies – including the USSR – launched a number of offensives across Europe, with varying degrees of success, all of which eroded Nazi control. Although the landings succeeded in creating an Allied entry point into Nazi-controlled Europe, it was still very much a 'first step'. It would take another year before the western Allies would reach their journey's end. However, the 'first step' is often the most important in any journey.

Historiography

"The mythologies never capture things that well. There is one thing that every historian says at least six times a day: "Well, it was more complicated than that." That applies equally well here."

Professor Jennifer Sessions

Interview by Matt Kelly: Historians: The Full Story of D-Day is More Complex Than the Myth

Where to find out more

Neptune: The Allied Invasion of Europe and the D-Day Landings
Craig L. Symonds

The Longest Day
Cornelius Ryan

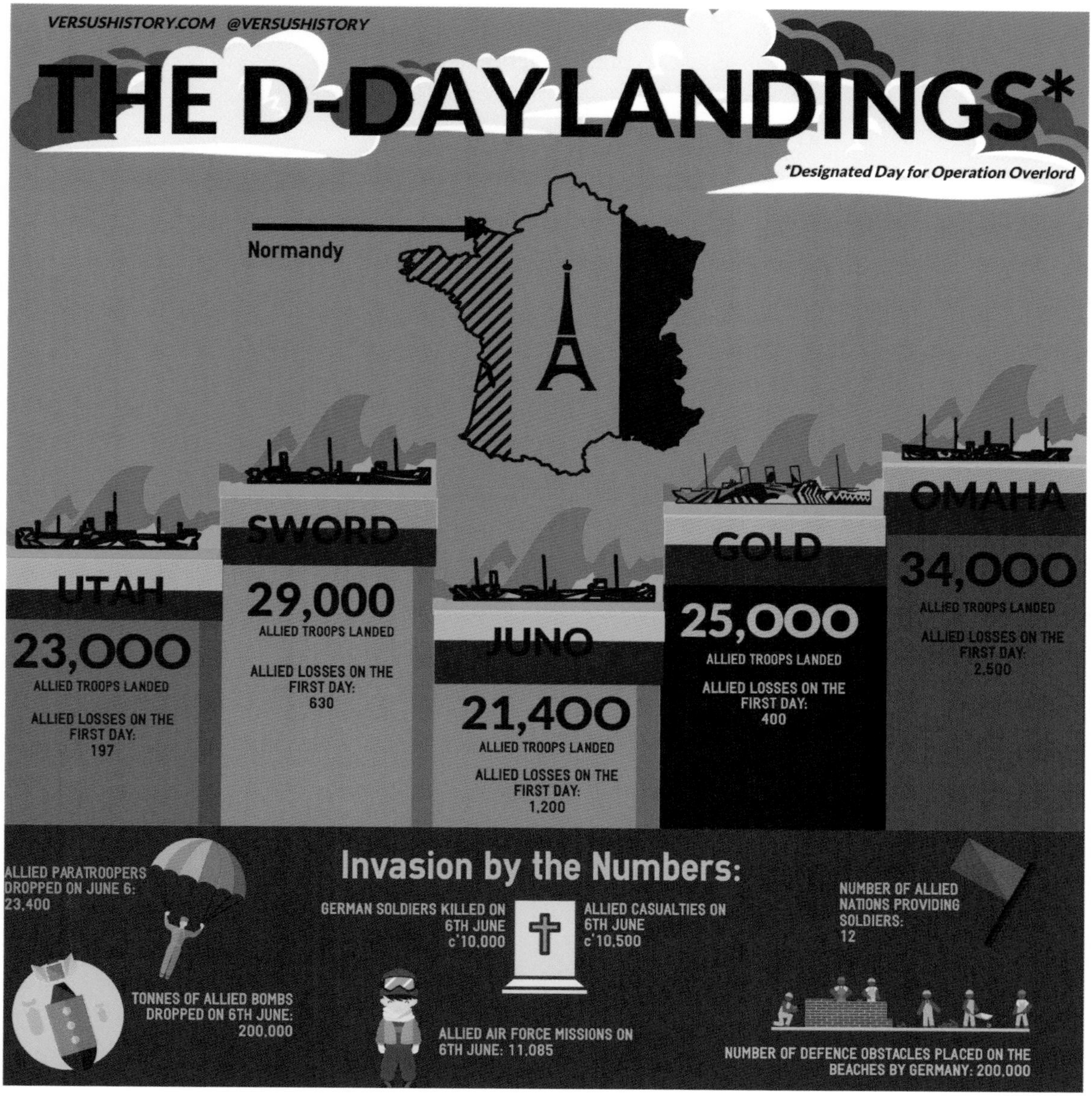
VERSUSHISTORY.COM @VERSUSHISTORY
THE D-DAY LANDINGS*
*Designated Day for Operation Overlord
Normandy
UTAH
23,000
ALLIED TROOPS LANDED
ALLIED LOSSES ON THE FIRST DAY: 197
SWORD
29,000
ALLIED TROOPS LANDED
ALLIED LOSSES ON THE FIRST DAY: 630
JUNO
21,400
ALLIED TROOPS LANDED
ALLIED LOSSES ON THE FIRST DAY: 1,200
GOLD
25,000
ALLIED TROOPS LANDED
ALLIED LOSSES ON THE FIRST DAY: 400
OMAHA
34,000
ALLIED TROOPS LANDED
ALLIED LOSSES ON THE FIRST DAY: 2,500
Invasion by the Numbers:
ALLIED PARATROOPERS DROPPED ON JUNE 6: 23,400
GERMAN SOLDIERS KILLED ON 6TH JUNE c'10,000
ALLIED CASUALTIES ON 6TH JUNE c'10,500
NUMBER OF ALLIED NATIONS PROVIDING SOLDIERS: 12
TONNES OF ALLIED BOMBS DROPPED ON 6TH JUNE: 200,000
ALLIED AIR FORCE MISSIONS ON 6TH JUNE: 11,085
NUMBER OF DEFENCE OBSTACLES PLACED ON THE BEACHES BY GERMANY: 200,000

Hitler's red scare

Overview

When Hitler ordered the attack on Stalingrad (now renamed Volgograd) in August 1942, he did so with the firm belief that, after the Luftwaffe had rained bombs down from the sky and razed large sections of the city to the ground, the battle would be swift and decisive. The Battle of Stalingrad was anything but swift, though it *was* decisive, just not in the way that Hitler had hoped. Lasting just over five months, and costing over a million lives, the bloodiest battle of the war – perhaps in history – forced the Wehrmacht into a retreat and served Hitler with his first real military defeat.

Significance

If ever an event could be described as a *turning point*, the Battle of Stalingrad should be. To many, it is viewed as the most significant turning point in the history of warfare; to some, it is the most significant turning point in the modern era. It was certainly the bloodiest. Up until the defeat at Stalingrad, the German war machine had met with success after success, steamrollering most of Europe and parts of north Africa. Apart from the defeat at El Alamein by the British in November 1941, which saw the relatively small number of 50,000 German soldiers lost, the Battle of Stalingrad saw the Red Army and the Russian people serve up an existential defeat to Hitler's military from which it would never recover. As the frost-bitten Wehrmacht was pushed back through territory it had previously occupied, news of the loss spread throughout the world and destroyed the veneer of invincibility that had previously been so resistant to damage. Stalingrad was the beginning of the end for the Third Reich.

Historiography

"The point about the Battle of Stalingrad was that it was the psychological turning point of the war."

Antony Beevor
Interview by Coilin O'Connor: A Victory of Courage and Coercion: British Historian on Stalingrad's Legacy

Where to find out more

The Year of Stalingrad
Alexander Werth

Stalingrad
Vasily Grossman

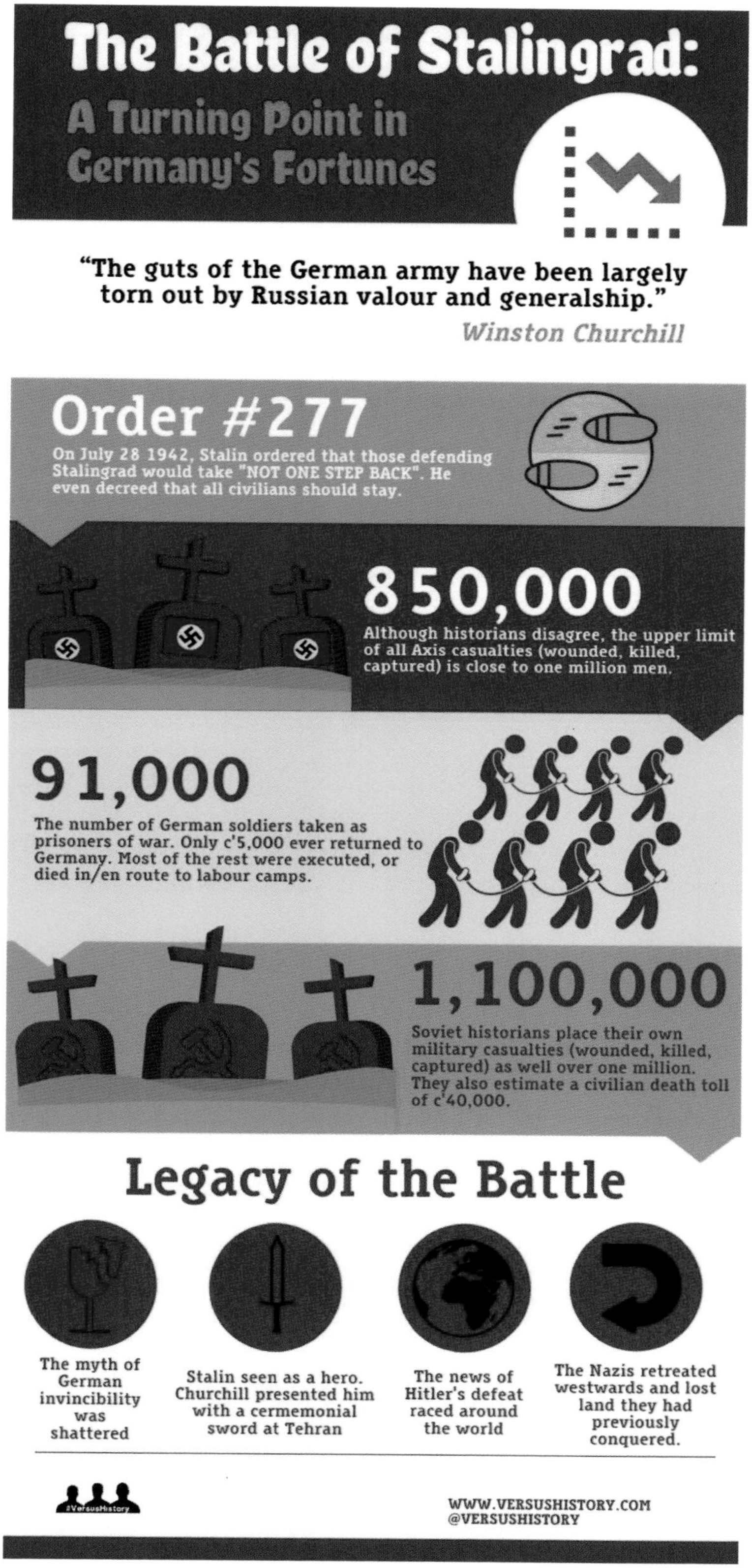
The Battle of Stalingrad:
A Turning Point in Germany's Fortunes
"The guts of the German army have been largely torn out by Russian valour and generalship."
Winston Churchill
Order #277
On July 28 1942, Stalin ordered that those defending Stalingrad would take "NOT ONE STEP BACK". He even decreed that all civilians should stay.
850,000
Although historians disagree, the upper limit of all Axis casualties (wounded, killed, captured) is close to one million men.
91,000
The number of German soldiers taken as prisoners of war. Only c'5,000 ever returned to Germany. Most of the rest were executed, or died in/en route to labour camps.
1,100,000
Soviet historians place their own military casualties (wounded, killed, captured) as well over one million. They also estimate a civilian death toll of c'40,000.
Legacy of the Battle
The myth of German invincibility was shattered
Stalin seen as a hero. Churchill presented him with a cermemonial sword at Tehran
The news of Hitler's defeat raced around the world
The Nazis retreated westwards and lost land they had previously conquered.
#VersusHistory
WWW.VERSUSHISTORY.COM
@VERSUSHISTORY

1945: the road to ruin

Overview

By 1945, it was clear to most observers that Germany was in retreat; some even foresaw the imminent end of the Third Reich. Hitler, ensconced in his underground *Führerbunker* – located not fifteen minutes' walk from the Reichstag Building – continued to issue military directives to his commanders who were becoming increasingly unwilling to carry them out. Although rarely insubordinate to his face, Hitler's generals understood the grim realities of the war; many knew the end was nigh and began trying to mitigate the impending tragedies of losing the war. Hitler was unable to recognise the same realities – that Germany was being squeezed, inexorably, by the Allies from the west and the east.

Significance

Hitler's brutal and lamentable intransigence in recognising that Germany was finished, meant that the war continued, perhaps unnecessarily, for the first five months of 1945. As the western Allies – Britain, America, Canada and what was left of the French forces – pushed the German Wehrmacht back towards Berlin, they swept up millions of soldiers who surrendered. The USSR made similar advances, but from the east. The Red Army, compelled by Stalin, and by the recent memories of Nazi atrocities on their own soil, took prisoners in name only as they moved westwards; they were prepared to mete out their own style of violent – and sometimes vile – justice on the Germans and those who collaborated with them. When Hitler killed himself in that Berlin bunker, the war – at least in Europe – all but came to an end. In truth, for Germany, it had been over for months.

Historiography

"The Russians, who'd suffered terribly from what the Germans did to their country, arrived in Germany bent upon a terrible revenge."

Max Hastings
Interview on NPR: Remembering the Final Days of World War II

Where to find out more

The Fall of Berlin 1945
Antony Beevor

The Rise and Fall of the Third Reich
William L. Shirer

THE ROAD TO GERMAN DEFEAT 1945

May 7th 1945

General Alfred Jodl surrenders all German forces to the Allies. The next day the war in Europe officially ends, celebrated as VE- Day.

April 29th - May 6th 1945

German forces surrender in Italy, Berlin, North West Germany, Denmark, Netherlands, Bavaria, and Breslau. Hermann Göring surrenders on 6th May.

April 30th 1945

With the Battle for Berlin over, and Soviet troops less than 500 metres from the Führerbunker, Hitler and his new wife, Eva Braun, commit suicide.

April 29th 1945

Germany's war ally, Italy, surrenders all Italian armed forces. One day earlier. Fascist leader, Mussolini, had been executed by Italian Partisans.

January - April 1945

As the Allies move in on Germany from the east and the west, vast numbers of prisoners are captured: over 800,000 surrender in the east, and over 2 million are captured in the west.

VersusHistory.com @versushistory

The key...

Studying any period of history is a challenge. Studying a period of history that involves a particular nomenclature – system of language – is an even greater challenge. Studying a period of history that has a particular nomenclature in an *unfamiliar language* is the greatest challenge. If the German language is unfamiliar to you – the reader – then the following few pages might help you navigate some of the key words and terms that are often used in the study of this period. This is not an exhaustive glossary – that would require a book in itself – but it will give the reader a sample of terminology that is specific to this period that can be used to unlock greater understanding.

The infographic opposite can be accessed using the QR Code below, whilst the glossary itself can be downloaded using the QR Code on the infographic itself. Go unlock your understanding.

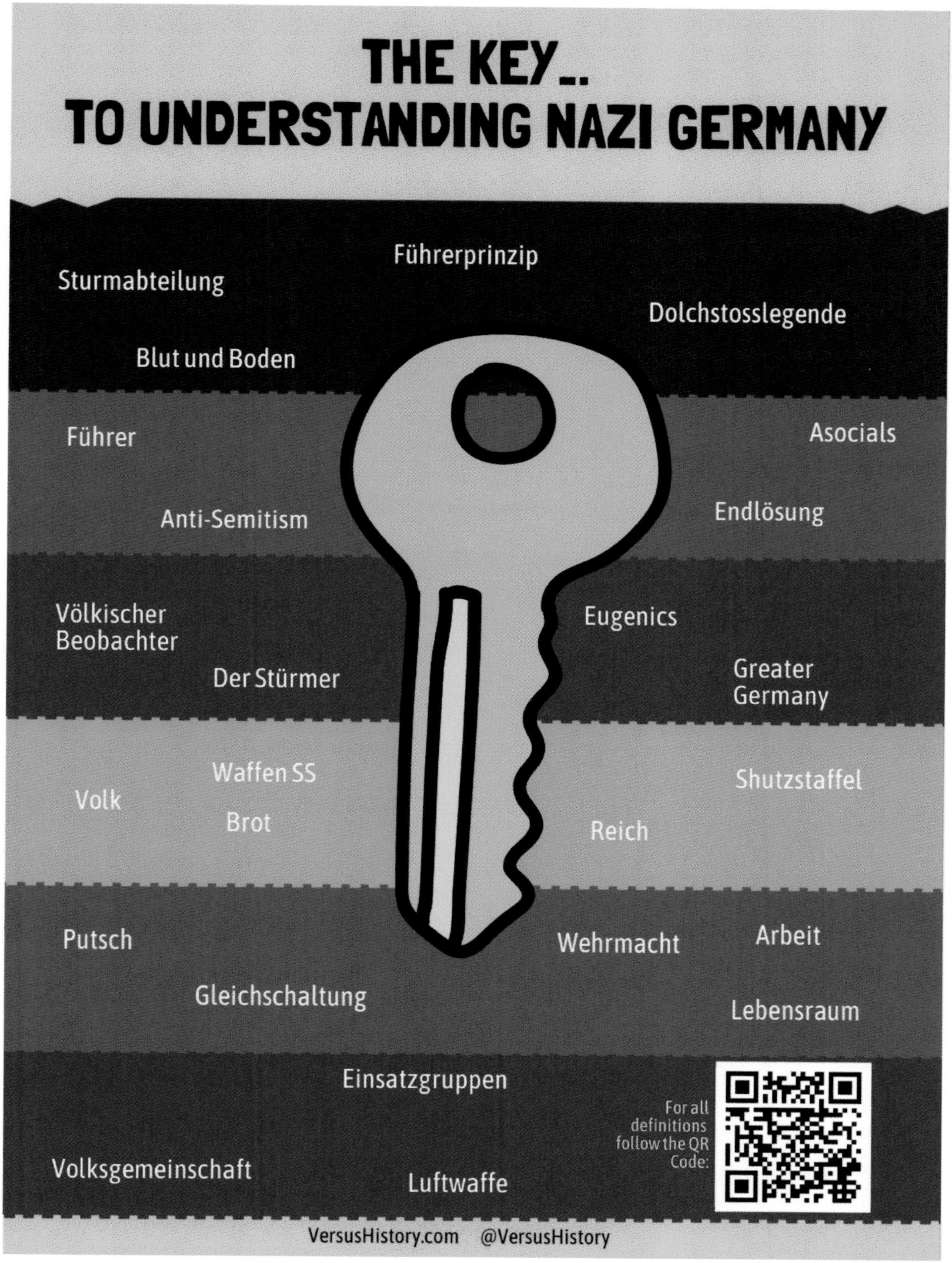
THE KEY..
TO UNDERSTANDING NAZI GERMANY
Führerprinzip
Sturmabteilung
Dolchstosslegende
Blut und Boden
Führer
Asocials
Anti-Semitism
Endlösung
Völkischer Beobachter
Eugenics
Der Stürmer
Greater Germany
Waffen SS
Volk
Shutzstaffel
Brot
Reich
Putsch
Wehrmacht
Arbeit
Gleichschaltung
Lebensraum
Einsatzgruppen
For all definitions follow the QR Code:
Volksgemeinschaft
Luftwaffe
VersusHistory.com @VersusHistory

Anti-Semitism

Hatred for Members of the Jewish Race.

Hitler's anti-Semitism became the basis for much of Nazi policy once in power. Since he was the ideological centre of the Party, anti-Semitism became a core tenet of National Socialism and it led to the racist atrocities committed by the Third Reich.

Asocials

People in Nazi Germany who were considered as existing outside of the natural order of productive society.

Thousands of people were condemned to detention, sterilisation, hard-labour, and death on the grounds that they did not conform to the Nazi notion of 'productivity' within the Volksgemeinschaft. For Hitler, 'productivity' was a catch-all term that required an economic, cultural, ideological, racial, and physical contribution to the Third Reich.

Der Stürmer

The Stormer/The Striker/The Attacker

Weekly tabloid-style newspaper published from 1923 until the end of World War Two. It was published by Julius Streicher and played a significant role in promoting Nazi propaganda. The newspaper was virulently anti-Semitic and pushed criminally racist conspiracy theories targeted at Germany's minorities. The tagline which appeared at the bottom of the front page of every issue read, "Die Juden sind unser Unglück!" – "The Jews are our misfortune".

Einsatzgruppen

Task Forces/Deployment Groups.

Paramilitary death squads of the Schutzstaffel (SS) with responsibility for the mass killings of peoples in German-occupied Europe. Overseen by Heinrich Himmler and Reinhard Heydrich, the Einsatzgruppen were also instrumental in the Final Solution.

Arbeit

Work/Labour.

A common German word that took on a different meaning under the Nazis – because of its association with forced labour in the concentration camps and murder in the extermination camps. Arbeit macht frei (work makes you free) infamously greeted the inmates of Auschwitz death camp.

Blut and Boden

Blood and Soil.

A propaganda and policy slogan that gained traction with German nationalists and racialists. The Blood referred to that of 'pure' Germans and 'Soil' to the geography from which those 'pure' Germans would come: the rural areas. Hitler believed the 'purest' Germans were those who had not had their bloodlines diluted by marrying 'inferior' races, such as the Jews; these Germans were to be found in the rural areas – where racial mixing was rarer than in the urban areas.

Dolchstosslegende

Stab-in-the-Back-Myth.

A term popularised by Field Marshal Paul von Hindenburg who believed that the German loss in World War One was not down to military failures or a lack of fighting spirit by her troops, but by treacherous forces within the government at home. The Nazis conflated this myth with anti-Semitic conspiracy theories as well as linking it to the untrustworthiness of the Weimar government.

Endlösung

Final Solution.

Nazi Germany's plan for the systematic genocide of Europe's Jews.

Eugenics

The process by which animals are bred to ensure their offspring contain specific and desired inherited genetic characteristics.

The erroneous Nazi belief in the racial superiority of northern Europeans led them to devise policies whereby so-called 'inferior' races would be bred out of existence, leaving only those with the 'desirable' Nordic characteristics to repopulate Europe.

Führer

Leader.

The word Führer is a perfectly normal word in German when used outside of the political realm and in a compound form. It denotes somebody of seniority and experience in a certain area, e.g. Spielführer means 'Team captain'. However, its use is avoided in contemporary German politics and is most widely known outside of Germany because of its association with Adolf Hitler.

Führerprinzip

Leadership Principle.

Refers to the manner of leadership in the Third Reich which saw Hitler as the absolute authority; the Führer's words were to be made law and all policies, decisions and ministries should work towards carrying out his proclamations. Within the NSDAP the Führerprinzip was established in 1926 at the Bamberg Conference whereby Hitler demanded absolute authority within the Party.

Gleichschaltung

Coordination.

The word used to describe the process by which all aspects of German life would be 'Nazified'. Gleichschaltung, was the basis for Hitler's attempt at the totalitarian control of Germany.

Greater Germany

Großgermanisches Reich/ Greater Germanic Reich.

The official name of the pan-Germanic state that Hitler sought to create. It would be a German super-state that would encompass much of Europe and contain all Germanic peoples. Obviously, in order to create such a thing, war would be inevitable.

Lebensraum

Living Space/Living Room.

Term used by the Nazis when explaining the apparent need for more territory to accommodate the growing German population. According to Hitler, Lebensraum was to be found in the lands of eastern Europe and Russia. Into these lands, once they had been 'vacated' of indigenous populations, Germans would be migrated.

Luftwaffe

German Airforce until 1945.

The aerial branch of the Wehrmacht (armed forces).

Putsch

Coup/Violent attempt to overthrow a government.

During the years 1918-23, there were several attempts to overthrow the new Weimar government. One of these, of course, was the Munich Putsch, led by Hitler.

www.VersusHistory.com @VersusHistory

Reich

Realm/Empire.

The Nazis attempted to portray their rule as a continuation of a proud German history that had conquered Europe, in what they retrospectively termed the First and Second Reichs. The Nazi Third Reich was to be, as Hitler would have it, the next manifestation of Germany's dominance of Europe. This Third Reich would last for a thousand years. It lasted twelve.

Schutzstaffel

Protection Squad/Blackshirts.

Nazi paramilitary organisation that started as a security team given the task of protecting prominent Nazis at NSDAP rallies. Under the leadership of Heinrich Himmler it grew to become the most prominent agent of terror and surveillance in Nazi occupied Europe.

Sturmabteilung

Storm Detachment/SA/Brownshirts.

The original Nazi paramilitary unit. Responsible for protecting Hitler, disrupting opposition meetings, providing security for National Socialist rallies. De facto head was Ernst Röhm. Its leadership was purged in the Night of the Long Knives in 1934 and its influence/membership reduced sharply thereafter.

Volk

A simple German word meaning people.

Used by nationalists in Germany to describe a racially, ethnically, and culturally distinct people who should form the foundation of the Third Reich.

Völkischer Beobachter

People's Observer.

The weekly newspaper of the National Socialist German Worker's Party (NSDAP/Nazi Party).

Volksgemeinschaft

People's Community.

A term used frequently in German history to promote the notion of a national community without hierarchy and class, working towards national success. It was adopted by the Nazis who included a racial element. They used it as a means to, and the final product of, their Third Reich. All 'racially pure' Germans would form a crucial element of this Volksgemeinschaft and, in turn, they would – through their efforts – help create the next incarnation of historical German supremacy.

Waffen-SS

Weapon-Schutzstaffel.

The military wing of the Nazi Party's Schutzstaffel (SS).

Wehrmacht

Defence Force/Armed Forces.

The name for the Nazi armed forces which replaced the traditionally used Reichswehr. It included the Heer (army), the Kriegsmarine (navy), and the Luftwaffe (airforce).

www.VersusHistory.com @VersusHistory

THE KEY...TO UNDERSTANDING NAZI GERMANY

Anti-Semitism
Hatred for Members of the Jewish Race.
Hitler's anti-Semitism became the basis for much of Nazi policy once in power. Since he was the ideological centre of the Party, anti-Semitism became a core tenet of National Socialism and it led to the racist atrocities committed by the Third Reich.

Arbeit
Work/Labour.
A common German word that took on a different meaning under the Nazis – because of its association with forced labour in the concentration camps and murder in the extermination camps. *Arbeit macht frei* (work makes you free) infamously greeted the inmates of Auschwitz death camp.

Asocials
People in Nazi Germany who were considered as existing outside of the natural order of productive society.
Thousands of people were condemned to detention, sterilisation, hard-labour, and death on the grounds that they did not conform to the Nazi notion of 'productivity' within the Volksgemeinschaft. For Hitler, 'productivity' was a catch-all term that required an economic, cultural, ideological, racial, and physical contribution to the Third Reich.

Blut and Boden
Blood and Soil.
A propaganda and policy slogan that gained traction with German nationalists and racialists. The *Blood* referred to that of 'pure' Germans and '*Soil*' to the geography from which those 'pure' Germans would come: the rural areas. Hitler believed the 'purest' Germans were those who had not had their bloodlines diluted by marrying 'inferior' races, such as the Jews; these Germans were to be found in the rural areas – where racial mixing was rarer than in the urban areas.

Der Stürmer
The Stormer/The Striker/The Attacker
Weekly tabloid-style newspaper published from 1923 until the end of World War Two. It was published by Julius Streicher and played a significant role in promoting Nazi propaganda. The newspaper was virulently anti-Semitic and pushed criminally racist conspiracy theories targeted at Germany's minorities. The tagline which appeared at the bottom of the front page of every issue read, *"Die Juden sind unser Unglück!" – "The Jews are our misfortune"*.

Dolchstosslegende
Stab-in-the-Back-Myth.
A term popularised by Field Marshal Paul von Hindenburg who believed that the German loss in World War One was not down to military failures or a lack of fighting spirit by her troops, but by treacherous forces within the government at home. The Nazis conflated this myth with anti-Semitic conspiracy theories as well as linking it to the untrustworthiness of the Weimar government.

Einsatzgruppen
Task Forces/Deployment Groups.
Paramilitary death squads of the *Schutzstaffel* (SS) with responsibility for the mass killings of peoples in German-occupied Europe. Overseen by Heinrich Himmler and Reinhard Heydrich, the *Einsatzgruppen* were also instrumental in the Final Solution.

Endlösung
Final Solution.
Nazi Germany's plan for the systematic genocide of Europe's Jews.

Eugenics
The process by which animals are bred to ensure their offspring contain specific and desired inherited genetic characteristics.
The erroneous Nazi belief in the racial superiority of northern Europeans led them to devise policies whereby so-called 'inferior' races would be bred out of existence, leaving only those with the 'desirable' Nordic characteristics to repopulate Europe.

Führer
Leader.
The word *Führer* is a perfectly normal word in German when used outside of the political realm and in a compound form. It denotes somebody of seniority and experience in a certain area, e.g. *Spielführer* means 'Team captain'. However, its use is avoided in contemporary German politics and is most widely known outside of Germany because of its association with Adolf Hitler.

Führerprinzip
Leadership Principle.
Refers to the manner of leadership in the Third Reich which saw Hitler as the absolute authority; the Führer's words were to be made law and all policies, decisions and ministries should work towards carrying out his proclamations. Within the NSDAP the *Führerprinzip* was established in 1926 at the Bamberg Conference whereby Hitler demanded absolute authority within the Party.

Gleichschaltung
Coordination.
The word used to describe the process by which all aspects of German life would be 'Nazified'. Gleichschaltung, was the basis for Hitler's attempt at the totalitarian control of Germany.

Greater Germany
Großgermanisches Reich/ Greater Germanic Reich.
The official name of the pan-Germanic state that Hitler sought to create. It would be a German super-state that would encompass much of Europe and contain *all* Germanic peoples. Obviously, in order to create such a thing, war would be inevitable.

Lebensraum
Living Space/Living Room.
Term used by the Nazis when explaining the apparent need for more territory to accommodate the growing German population. According to Hitler, Lebensraum was to be found in the lands of eastern Europe and Russia. Into these lands, once they had been 'vacated' of indigenous populations, Germans would be migrated.

Luftwaffe
German Airforce until 1945.
The aerial branch of the Wehrmacht (armed forces).

Putsch
Coup/Violent attempt to overthrow a government.
During the years 1918-23, there were several attempts to overthrow the new Weimar government. One of these, of course, was the Munich Putsch, led by Hitler.

Reich
Realm/Empire.
The Nazis attempted to portray their rule as a continuation of a proud German history that had conquered Europe, in what they retrospectively termed the *First* and *Second Reichs.* The Nazi Third Reich was to be, as Hitler would have it, the next manifestation of Germany's dominance of Europe. This Third Reich would last for a thousand years. It lasted twelve.

Schutzstaffel
Protection Squad/Blackshirts.
Nazi paramilitary organisation that started as a security team given the task of protecting prominent Nazis at NSDAP rallies. Under the leadership of Heinrich Himmler it grew to become the most prominent agent of terror and surveillance in Nazi occupied Europe.

Sturmabteilung
Storm Detachment/SA/Brownshirts.
The original Nazi paramilitary unit. Responsible for protecting Hitler, disrupting opposition meetings, providing security for National Socialist rallies. De facto head was Ernst Röhm. Its leadership was purged in the Night of the Long Knives in 1934 and its influence/membership reduced sharply thereafter.

Volk
A simple German word meaning people.
Used by nationalists in Germany to describe a racially, ethnically, and culturally distinct people who should form the foundation of the Third Reich.

Völkischer Beobachter
People's Observer.
The weekly newspaper of the National Socialist German Worker's Party (NSDAP/Nazi Party).

Volksgemeinschaft
People's Community.
A term used frequently in German history to promote the notion of a national community without hierarchy and class, working towards national success. It was adopted by the Nazis who included a racial element. They used it as a means to, and the final product of, their Third Reich. All 'racially pure' Germans would form a crucial element of this Volksgemeinschaft and, in turn, they would – through their efforts – help create the next incarnation of historical German supremacy.

Waffen-SS
Weapon-Schutzstaffel.
The military wing of the Nazi Party's Schutzstaffel (SS).

Wehrmacht
Defence Force/Armed Forces.
The name for the Nazi armed forces which replaced the traditionally used Reichswehr. It included the *Heer* (army), the Kriegsmarine (navy), and the Luftwaffe (airforce).

Other works by Versus History

Amazon Bestseller:
33 Easy Ways to Improve Your History Essays:

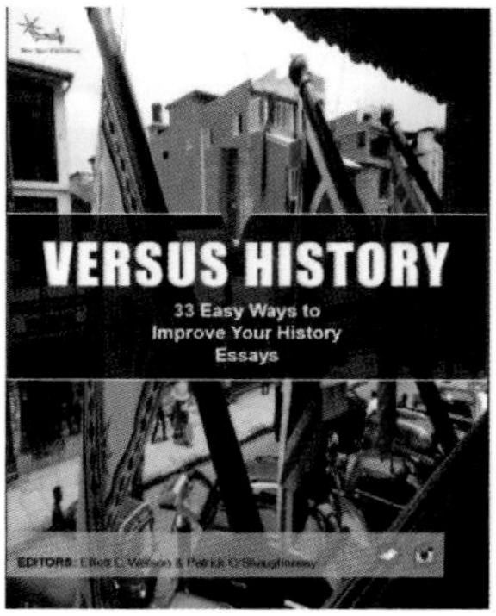

Amazon Bestseller:
Blowing up the Nazis: What you didn't know will blow your mind

University History Essays (and how to write them)

Lord Durham and the Canada Question:

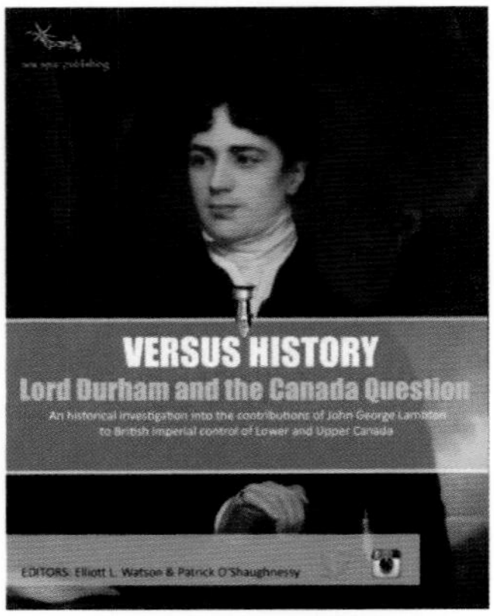

Don't forget our **Versus History Podcast**, available from wherever you download your podcasts.

Versus History are Conal Smith, Dr. Elliott L. Watson, and Patrick O'Shaughnessy.

Published by New Spur Publishing

First published 2020

For permission requests, please contact us at www.versushistory.com, elliottlwatson74@gmail.com, and prohistoricman@gmail.com.

Websites
www.versushistory.com
www.thecourseworkclub.com

Twitter:
@VersusHistory
@thelibrarian6
@prohistoricman

Instagram:
versushistory

Printed by Amazon Italia Logistica S.r.l.
Torrazza Piemonte (TO), Italy

12616176R20078